Literature
and
Culture

Literature and Culture

Sachidananda Mohanty

PRESTIGE

PRESTIGE BOOKS
3/28, East Patel Nagar
New Delhi 110 008

ISBN: 81-7551-113-3

Printed at Chaman Offset Press, New Delhi 110 002

CONTENTS

Towards a "Cultured Humanity"
Sri Aurobindo
9

Introduction
15

Why Cultural Travel?
18

On the Trail of D.H. Lawrence:
Taos, New Mexico, USA
24

A Literary Treasure House:
Humanities Research Centre,
Texas, Austin, USA
29

Subverting Hegemonic Histories:
Cairo, Egypt
34

An Easterner in Eastwood—I:
Nottinghamshire, UK, 1990
38

An Easterner in Eastwood—II:
Nottinghamshire, UK, 1999
42

A Crop of Writers at Cambridge:
Cambridge, UK
48

Small is Always Beautiful:
The Writers' Workshop Story
55

The School that D.H. Lawrence Went to
61

The Future of Literature
66

Education: Call for a New Definition
71

University as an Apex of Intellectual,
Creative Life
75

Savage Pilgrimage:
Relevance of D.H. Lawrence Today
80

Master of Campus Fiction:
David Lodge
85

A Literature of Their Own:
Early Literary Women of Orissa
90

Fulbright and International Education
101

The Virtue of Aloneness
106

Cracked Goodwill: Cultural Factors in Indo-U.S. Relationship
109

The Future of American Studies
116

Who's Afraid of Shakespeare?: The Bard in the Classroom
121

The Burden of the Past: The ICHR Controversy
123

Dreaming Indian: Acting as Writer?: The Importance of Regional Languages
127

The Social Vision of Sri Aurobindo
131

Literary Conversations

"Feminism Must Reach out to the World": Sandra Gilbert
136

Freedom and the Indian Diaspora Meena Alexander
145

The Best Words in Their Best Order Blake Morrison
155

A Wandering Writer Finds Home
Farrukh Dhondy
161

"The Deconstrutionist Era is Over"
Malcolm Bradbury
169

Out of the Shadows
Namita Gokhale
174

Translation as a Form of Negotiation
Susan Bassnett
179

"We Don't Sell Art in Our Culture"
Prafulla Mohanti
188

English Studies and Multiculturalism
Alastair Niven
195

Theatre: Reaching out to People
Mahesh Dattani
203

"A Good Translation is a Good Literary Text"
Piotr Kuhiwczak
211

Partition Revisited
Shiv K. Kumar
218

Creating an Alternative Universe
Sitakant Mahapatra
226

Dedicated

to

the memory

of

my mother,

Bidyut Prabha

Towards a "Cultured Humanity"

Commercialisation is still the heart of modern civilisation's sensational activism, is still its driving force. Modern education has not in the mass redeemed the sensational man; it has only made necessary to him things to which he was not formerly accustomed, mental activity and occupations, intellectual, and even aesthetic sensations, emotions of idealism. He still lives in the vital substratum, but he wants it stimulated from above. He requires an army of writers to keep him mentally occupied, and to provide some sort of intellectual pabulum for him. He has a thirst for general information of all kinds which he does not care for, or has not time to co-ordinate or assimilate.

The result has been to cheapen thought and art and literature, to make talent, and even genius run in the grooves of popular success, to put the writer and thinker and scientist very much in the position like that of the cultured Greek slave in a Roman household . . .

The highest mental life, in a word, has been democratised, sensationalised, activised, with both good and bad results. Through it all, the eye of faith can see perhaps that a crude but enormous change has begun. Thought and Knowledge, if not yet Beauty, can get a hearing, and even produce rapidly some large, vague, yet in the end effective will for their results; the mass of culture and of men who think and strive seriously to appreciate and to know has enormously increased behind all this surface veil of sensationalism, and even the sensational man has begun to undergo a process of transformation. Especially, new methods of education, new principles of society are beginning to come into the range of practical possibility, which will create perhaps one day that as yet unknown phenomenon, a race of men—not only a class—who have to some extent found and developed their mental selves, a cultured humanity.

Sri Aurobindo, "Civilisation and Culture," *The Human Cycle* (Pondicherry: Sri Aurobindo Ashram, 1962), pp. 117-18.

ACKNOWLEDGEMENTS

Several individuals and institutions are responsible for the making of this book. Far too numerous and scattered as they are, it would be impossible to thank them individually. This list ought to be taken, therefore, as representative, and not exhaustive, of the set of benefactors. I wish to thank, in particular, the following:

- The editors of the following periodicals/newspapers for their kind permission to reprint the articles: *The Hindu*, *The Indian Express*, *Deccan Herald*, *The Statesman*, *Deccan Chronicle*, *Span* Magazine, *A.P. Times* and *Newstime*.
- Nirmala Lakshman, Malini Parthasarathy, Nanda Kumar, Shalini Arun and colleagues at *The Hindu*'s magazine/literary supplements, Mini Krishnan of Macmillan India, Arun Shourie (then of *The Indian Express*), Aditi De, Sudha Ramachandran and S. Sugata and Jayalakshmi of *Deccan Herald*, Manoj Das (then *of The Heritage*), and Amar Singh of *Oriya Aurovillian* for the interest they took in my work and for having offered me a forum in the first place.
- My teachers who have had a formative influence upon my writing career Hyderabad Hyderabad—Kishor Gandhi, Nirod Baran, Tehmi behn, Priti Ghosh, S. Nagarajan, Shiv K. Kumar, S. Viswanathan and R.K. Gupta.
- The Chairman and all my colleagues at the Department of English, University of Hyderabad, as well as my students and research scholars for providing a stimulating environment for work. Each of my colleagues, in his or her own special way, has been a valuable presence.
- Friends and colleagues at sister institutes s;uch as IACIS (formerly American Research Centre), the CIEFL, Osmania

University, USEFI, USIS and British Council for their invaluable support and constant encouragement.

- The scholars and literary luminaries I had the good fortune to meet and talk to in the U.K., U.S., Europe, the Middle East and South East Asia.
- My father Panchanan Mohanty, uncle Sanatan Mohanty, and other family members for being a perennial source of encouragement.
- Makarand and Sarina Paranjape, Suman Bala, Mamuni, Jimi, Tutun Mukherjee, Ranjana Harish and Panchanan Dalai.
- Dr. R.K. and Mrs. Usha Dhawan for their generosity
- Prestige Publishers for readily taking up this work for publication.
- Nicolétte Sharma for her sense of care and attention to detail. She showed exemplary professionalism in turning out a beautiful manuscript!
- Raja and Nagarajan for secretarial assistance at the Department of English.
- My late mother Bidyut Prabha, a renowned poet, for her idealism and commitment to literary values.
- Finally, my countless readers. It is they who keep me going, as always!

Hyderabad **Sachidananda Mohanty**

Introduction

We live in an age of paradoxes where the Orwellian double talk, once menacing, has become domesticated, routine wisdom! And so, public schools signifying community learning must stand for elite, commercial education. Similarly, the more astronomical the prize money for a Booker or a Crossword Literary Prize, the lesser is the number of the reading public, and equally, our "public discourse" must increasingly address an audience minority in character.

Nowhere is this painful duality, this gross contradiction, more manifest than in the interface between Literature and Society. As culture gives in more and more to commerce, business and technology, then public criticism of literature and culture becomes more and more scarce. The figure of the "poet laureate" as a Tennysonian iconic figure addressing fellowmen, or an Arnoldian critical voice addressing issues of his day becomes only a relic of a bygone era!

Thus, the cultural critic of today, unlike his predecessors like a Matthew Arnold, Edmund Wilson, Lionel Trilling, F.R. Leavis or a Raymond Williams, is a rarity today. He does not have their insight, wisdom and passion. No doubt, their legacy continues even today, in the Sunday Literary Supplements of newspapers, periodicals, the review journals and book talks, but clearly these are only pale shadows, acts of mimicry rather than the real thing!

Not surprisingly, therefore, so much of literary journalism today sounds disappointingly and monotonously similar. Highly verbose, personalised, and full of self-conscious rhetoric and pedantry, this criticism seldom serves the twin purposes of delight and instruction—the traditional objectives of all critical enquiry. Nor is the critic sufficiently broad-based, endowed with observation and empathy to comment on literary texts, personalities and contexts. The journals, in their mad pursuit of populism, generate more of sensational heat than the light of understanding. There are honourable exceptions to this rule. It is these that hold out hope for the future of literary journalism.

The essays, literary conversations and travel pieces that I offer here, all affirm the crucial importance of the literary critic in our complex world today. They assume that literature is not a mere pastime for the leisure class or the idle rich. It is central to our life and adds meaning to our humdrum existence. Therefore, it is not the absence of the audience that we must mourn today as the disappearance of the critic, or what Edward Said calls the public intellectual. This is the direction in which literary journalism must go if it wishes to find its real métier.

II

The book is divided into two sections. Section I brings in essays related to literature and culture, and Section II deals with literary conversations. Nearly all the articles included here were published at the national level.

The first section opens with an overview called "Why Cultural Travel?" This is logically followed by a series—the search for D.H. Lawrence's trail at Taos, New Mexico; a narrative about the Humanities Research Centre at Texas, Austin; followed by a memorable meeting with Edward Said at Cairo. Then there are two literary travel pieces related to Eastwood, UK, and the birthplace of D.H. Lawrence. The two accounts are mediated by a gap of eight years. After this, a notable event is swiftly brought in—a conference at Cambridge, UK, which chronicles meetings with celebrity writers such as David Lodge, Malcolm Bradbury, Doris Lessing, Salman Rushdie, George Steiner, and others. Then there is Professor P. Lal and the Writers' Workshop story called "Small is Always Beautiful."

The next lot offers a set of reflective essays. The topics here all relate to contemporary literature and culture and address pressing issues. They range from the Future of Literature; A New Definition of Education; University as an Apex of Intellectual Life; The Relevance of D.H. Lawrence Today; The Emerging Genre of Campus Fiction; Early Literary Women of Orissa; Fulbright and International Education; The Virtue of Aloneness; Cultural Factors in Indo-American Cultural Relationship; The Bard in the Classroom; The Controversy over the Writing of History; The Importance of Regional Languages; and finally, The Social Vision of Sri Aurobindo.

Throughout, I have attempted to avoid a polemical style, I eschew the tempting desire to adopt a binary approach to cultural issues and score points with rival points of view. I believe that the issues, complex as they are, call for a balanced and nuanced response rather than dogmatic views that foist simplistic solutions in black and white. True liberalism clearly believes in seeing truth in many approaches. It does not demonise opponents and/or trivialise their arguments. It believes in what Patrick J. Hill aptly calls a conversation of respect among people holding rival points of view.

Section II comprises a set of literary conversations with celebrity writers and thinkers—Sandra Gilbert, Meena Alexander, Blake Morrison, Farrukh Dhondy, Malcolm Bradbury, Namita Gokhale, Susan Bassnett, Prafulla Mohanti, Alastair Niven, Mahesh Dattani, Piotr Kuhiwczak, Shiv K. Kumar, and Sitakant Mahapatra.

Culture in today's world has become a sham, a philistinism, the dance of a monkey on a computer keyboard. It must rediscover another image of itself, a vision rooted to the future of man and human possibilities.

Why Cultural Travel?

The desire for cultural travel stems from the ceaseless human urge for exploration, inscribed in all the great literatures of the world.

To know other countries is not to belittle but enlarge our own country and to help it to a greater power of its own being.

Sri Aurobindo, *The Future Poetry*

If we were to think of one single term that would sum up the sustained and near-universal drive for cultural travel throughout the world, ever since recorded history, it would perhaps be the ceaseless human urge for exploration. The drive for exploration is an insistent fact of life, constantly observed. It is repeatedly inscribed in all great literatures of the world—the Miltonic Adam looking down on the beatific earth, Ulysses' ceaseless voyages to seek, to conquer, and not to yield, Prospero's magical creations in Shakespeare's island of imagination, Rasselas' yearning to leave the "Happy Valley," the epic journeys of a Dante and Virgil; or Nachiketa and Orpheus' entry into the World of the Dead. Similarly, the great Middle Eastern narratives of the Arabian Nights and Sinbad the Sailor, the travels of the spiritual pilgrim in the East, the time travellers of H.G. Wells, or the scientific adventurers of Jules Vernes' fantasy world—all underlie the universal desire for travel. It must be Man's deep idealism and endless longings that make him a perpetually dissatisfied wayfarer.

There is an important distinction, however, between cultural travel and exchange activity. Exchange suggests reciprocation and mutuality. Few travels of the past were in this sense reciprocal. The primacy of the West in terms of technology and resources clearly meant that sponsored travels and visits could be seldom returned; all travel basically entailed a one-way traffic.

The typical exchange scholar in this sense is an iconic explorer of an alien culture. Today's exchange visitor is a specialised traveller or explorer. He is conferred status and legitimacy through peer group selection, backed by internationally recognised bodies. He partakes of a package of foreign currency, air travel, institutional linkages, and accreditation. His travel is programmed and his exploration valorised. His itinerary covers Tokyo, London, New York and Honolulu—seats of economic, cultural and political power. His travel adds to self-esteem and acts as an index of his personal and professional advancement.

The exchange scholar today is the Faustus of the modern world, journeying through nations and cultures, hungering forever after knowledge. He is lionised by corporations and think tanks, governments, media, and citizen groups. He is the oracular voice, the crystal gazer into our dim future.

Yet, in a fundamental sense, exchange travel marks little break from the traditional practice. If the former is defined as travel with a mission through institutional support, then few significant explorations of the past would fail this litmus test—the patronage of the royal Spanish dynasty (of Ferdinand and Isabella) for Columbus' voyage into the New World, the Royal Society's support for the scientific expedition of Darwin's exciting sea voyages, Vasco da Gama's compulsive voyage to the Indies in search of spices and new trade routes, or the sponsored journey of Stanley into the Belgian Congo to locate the missing Dr. Livingstone . . .

The early "exchange scholars" to India and Egypt, significantly, came along with an Alexander and a Napoleon. Conquerors! Megasthenes came to India as the envoy of Seleucus Nicator to the court of Chandragupta in 300 B.C. Several came with early Muslim invaders. The British East India Company added its own share of cultural visitors. Some of these visitors like Sombre, George Thomas and Benoit de Boigne and James Skinner, author Lester Hutchinson tells us, doubled up as military buccaneers. This is not to say that all travellers were motivated by the colonial spirit of cultural domination and appropriation. Indeed, there were many that were exceptions to the rule.

However, it testifies to the power of the subtle and not so subtle systems of rewards and punishments that the colonial administrative apparatus was capable of promoting cultural travel of a select kind. The collusion and coalition between the Colonial State and cultural institutions has been murky, sanctimonious and unsavoury. It is only now that we are beginning to understand the full extent of this nexus and its debilitating influence. The "willing" consent of the ruled vis-à-vis the "ruling ideas" offers us instructive lessons for understanding colonial travel, then as well as now. Narratives of the nineteenth century, both adventure as well as science fiction, repeatedly enact their stories on a soil that has an exotic and remote appeal. H. Rider Haggard's adventure novels, or Edgar Rice Burrough's celebrated Tarzan tales, set in the deepest Africa, recurrently punctuate the narrative with the mines of a King Solomon or civilisations of the Lost Whites in the heart of black Africa, just as Starship Enterprise's journey into outer space may represent the ultimate in Western imagination for conquest and colonisation.

It is only now that we are beginning to realise in India, thanks to the new scholarship in the field of women's, tribal, minorities', ethnic and Subaltern studies, the disturbingly pronounced use of the travel motif for cultural appropriation. The exhibition of our tribal population, their lifestyle and heritage through a safari-like travel results inevitably in cultural tourism, just as the display, sale and consumption of ethnic ware, through the pan-Indian cinema and advertisement campaigns, result in the commodification of culture. The passage of our exotic North East through the Republic Day tableaux may bolster the Indian State and its increasing reliance on the military, but it conceals the many wars of attrition and insurrection pervasive in our near-breakaway provinces.

Similarly, the sex appeal evoked by the exhilarating puff of a "Charms" cigarette, or the welcome sip of "Nescafe" always precede in cinemascope a controlled adventure in the cinematic jungle. The hero's destined encounter with a domestic man-eater forever wins gratitude from the maiden in distress around the glowing campfire. Just as the advertisement for "Bajaj Sunny," the popular two-wheeler, shows the white traveller merrily riding off into the distance as the group of blacks gape helpless, stupefied.

Thus, cultural exchange as a trope is not limited to the Fulbright, the Humboldt, or the Rockefeller alone. Whether we are aware or not, cultural exchange is a constantly ongoing activity, common to our everyday life. The field work that a researcher conducts, the trip that the Delhi-based planner makes to the hinterland of Bihar, the police beat that a crime reporter makes before filing his daily quota of crime stories—all are in a sense different forms of cultural travel. For in each case, the researcher, the planner, and the reporter enjoys an institutional position and a vantage point of power, a specific mission and term of reference. Each case involves the crossing of cultural frontiers and twilight zones related to cultural communities with their own subcultural medium, folklore, vocabulary and gestures. The irony is that the critic who makes an impassioned denunciation of cultural imperialism of a Western Foundation may be unaware of, or simply gloss over, his and her own blindness or insensitivity to the hierarchy of cultures in his or her own milieu.

Thus, cultural travel is not a matter of covering geographical space alone; it embraces emotive and psychic zones of our being, our dark recesses of memory and desire. It shows its identity through absence, especially in the intra-group context. Each time we ban a book or break a mosque, we mark our failure in cultural mediation. Restoring the harmony between the whole and the parts has been the primal challenge to Man. It is destined to remain the ultimate challenge as well. Cultural mediation has been our cross; it may well be our saviour.

It will be facile, however, to give a clarion call for cultural exchange without carefully mapping out the terrain we tread on. The world has changed beyond recognition ever since the signing of the Fulbright Act in 1946. The Cold War is gone and gone is the rationale for the old doctrines of balance of power. International travel through institutional support was a rarity in the forties. Today, the Fulbright occupies a very small proportion of all exchange activities. What is going to be the meaning of mutual exchange and mutual understanding when the Nation State in many parts of the world is either falling apart or increasingly lacks cohesion and stability? The Nation State, it has been aptly said, has become too small for the big problems. It faces the threat of an international system that is at once subnational and extranational. Some describe it as "an unnatural, even dysfunctional, unit for organising human activity and managing economic endeavour in a borderless world."

If totalitarian Communism of the Soviet kind has collapsed, it has not meant the end of history or the triumph of Capitalism. Historian Ainslie Embree considers the greatest challenge to democracies worldwide as the ongoing conflict between the majority versus the minority groups. The problem is simply how to organise through democratic means a hierarchy of loyalties. How indeed to serve allegiance at once to multiple loyalties—the family, the community, the nation, and the world—that democratic living basically entails? Again, if authority is legitimised power, then the irony is that the more we use power, the more we forfeit authority. A crisis in the modern Nation State is therefore a crisis of delegitimised authority. The ensuing spiral of delegitimisation appears fraudulent and the State becomes balkanised. There is a lesson here that the new Nation States must quickly learn. The majority must allow the groups' own version of history, language and culture. It is true that the balance between self-determination and national integration is always a delicate one, and in many parts of the world—Quebec, Bosnia, Kashmir and Jaffna—we lack viable answers.

We return to our earlier questions—-Why cultural exchange? And why cultural travel?

Cultural travel is important. Today more than ever before, for all the reasons cited. It is important, most of all, because of our knowledge of the world today.

We constantly hear phrases like information highway, cyber technology, and stellar travel. And yet, discord and dissonance seems to be our constant fate. We are deaf to the voice of the dispossessed "deeply desolate, like a cry and solitary like silent weeping." In our anger, we create new barriers, erect new walls that Edward Said warns us against. And we do not seem to possess "languages of suffering which are morally orienting." But we are not blind creatures of an irrevocable history, incapable of a moral choice of rebellion and reunion. "Our future is not in the stars but in our minds and hearts." Only dialogue can add meaning to this world and meditation redeem us from our fallen state.

On the Trail of D.H. Lawrence: Taos, New Mexico, USA

As a visiting Fulbright scholar (1990-91) at the University of Texas in Austin, and at Yale University in New Haven, Connecticut, I focused on "D.H. Lawrence's Contribution to the American Southwest." The highlight of my six-month stay in the United States was a trip to Taos, New Mexico, famed as much for its evocative beauty as for being D.H. Lawrence's second home. I also visited the cabin that Lawrence had renovated with the help of local American Indians.

It has been a week of bad weather. As the airplane takes off from Austin, Texas, through a dense cover of January fog and sleet, I close my eyes and send a silent prayer to the weather God. To a visitor heading toward the city of Taos in New Mexico for a three-day stay, nothing seems more important than the promise of sunshine. An hour later, as the plane approaches Albuquerque airport, the clouds suddenly part, revealing the majestic peaks of the Sangre de Cristo mountains.

As I head for the limo provided by Faust Transportation to take me to Taos, two hundred kilometres to the South, I find myself shivering. New Mexico is obviously colder and higher than Texas. "Come for skiing?" the driver asks me in Spanish-accented English. When I shake my head, he reasons, "Then you must be a writer." "Well, sort of," I mumble, hesitant to include myself in the company of D.H. Lawrence, who had made Taos his second home.

The drive from Albuquerque to Taos through Santa Fe takes about three hours and passes through some of the most beautiful sights I have seen. All around are mountains, encircling a vast open semidesert covered with a milk-white blanket of ice and snow.

At the outskirts of Taos, a lodging house proclaims its historical credentials with a cheeky signpost: "D.H. Lawrence may have slept here!"

It is 5 p.m. when the limo pulls up at Kachina Lodge, where Betsy Wolf, from the local Harwood Foundation of the University of New Mexico, receives me with a bag full of warm clothing. "I know you are from a warmer climate. This will come in handy," she explains with a smile. She drops me at the house of my host, Jacques Bassein, a French-American who is a housepainter and a musician. He and his wife, Marjorie, it turns out, had a stint learning Kathak from Prabha Marathe in Varanasi. We talk late into the night about Indian dance, French actor Gerard Depardeau, Lawrence, and the Gulf War.

I wake up to a glorious sunny day. Bassein's friend, David, a player of the Celtic harp and lover of Indian music and spirituality, drives me to the Rio Grande Canyon, past of a saga-covered Mesa. West of Taos, the bridge on the Rio Grande River is one of America's highest bridges, at two hundred metres. The river is now a trickle, but at other times of the year it swells with torrential rains, making it a delight for water-rafting daredevils.

I spend the next few hours looking around this quaint little town. Taos is unlike any other city I have seen in the United States. No shopping mall, no K-Marts, ne Sears and Roebuck, no Burger Kings, and no Texaco gas stations. Uniquely picturesque, Taos has always cast a magic spell upon artists and writers. Among its regular visitors have been art patroness Mabel Luhan, Lawrence's companion Dorothy Brett, novelist Aldous Huxley, music conductor Leopold Stokowski, poet Robinson Jeffers, and film stars Fred Astaire, Douglas Fairbanks, Gary Cooper and Janet Gaynor.

The town derives its name from an American-Indian word meaning "red willow." Today's Taos merges the cultural influences of the three groups who live here—the "Anglo," meaning the White Americans; the Spanish-Mexicans, and the Pueblo or the native American Indians. Taos' buildings reveal the influence of Spanish-Mexican designs; many of them are adobe houses made, as in India, of a mixture of straw and clay, which are intended to keep temperatures down during the blistering heat of summer. The plaza, or centre of town, is the site of the original Spanish settlement, then known as Don Fernando de Taos, founded in the 1790s. Dotting the plaza are little shops selling an assortment of souvenir items and artefacts made by the Pueblo Indians—exquisite kachina dolls, ceramics, necklaces of beads and mother of pearl—and several art galleries. Many painters, especially from the West Coast, have been lured by the landscape of Taos. The most spectacular of Taos' legacy, however, is La Fonda Hotel's collection of ten "infamous" paintings by D.H. Lawrence that are still banned in Great Britain.

Most people are not aware that Lawrence was a painter too. The best known of his paintings were done when he was in the company of the Huxleys in Italy. Exhibited for the first time in the Warren Gallery of London in 1929, thirteen of them were seized by the police. Judged obscene, they were ordered to be destroyed. But destruction was averted through a compromise that directed that the paintings be taken out of the country and that they never be put on exhibit again. After Lawrence's death in Vence, France, in 1930, the paintings followed his wife, Frieda, to Taos. After her death, her third husband, Angelo Ravagli, sold some of them to Saki Karavas, the owner of La Fonda Hotel.

I visited Karavas' study—after paying the admission fee of $1—to have a look at the paintings. The fleshy nudes may not conform accurately to human anatomy, but they suggest a playful sensuality. *Holy Family* is done in house paints. *Close Up Kiss* was apparently inspired by an Italian silent movie. *Kiowa Ranch New Mexico* portrays the ranch Mabel Luhan gave away to the Lawrences during their stay in Taos. There are other arresting canvases—*Red Willow Trees, Flight Back into Paradise, Fauns and Nymphs, Dance Sketch*, and *Rape of the Sabine Women*.

The next day, I see some more of Lawrence's Taos. Robert Ellis, Director of the Harwood Foundation, and his wife, Caroline, drive me to Lawrence's ranch and memorial high up in the mountains. The ranch is maintained by the University of New Mexico. We visit Lawrence's cabin, which he renovated with the help of local American Indians. Some distance away is Frieda's memorial to Lawrence—a simple altar containing his ashes. Outside on the crest is mounted the Phoenix, Lawrence's emblem. Frieda's tomb faces the entrance to Lawrence's memorial.

It is noon when we return to town. After a quick bite at the local Mexican restaurant, Betsy Wolf drives me to New Mexico's famous American-Indian village, Taos Pueblo, three kilometres north of Taos. The Taos Indians have lived at this site for nearly a thousand years, even after four hundred years of Spanish and Anglo presence. The mud and straw structures constitute some of the largest multi-storied pueblo buildings in the United States. Today, more than 1,900 Taos Indians live on Taos Pueblo lands. In 1970, the US Government returned 19,200 hectares of mountain land, including the sacred Blue Lake, to the Pueblo—a testimony to the successful struggle of the American Indians to preserve their cultural, economic and spiritual identity.

Right now it is Winter, so there are fewer festivals, but most of the year, the pueblo is full of song and dance—Turtle Dance on 1 January, Corn Dance on 3 May, Taos Pueblo Pow Wow on 2 July, Feast of San Gerommo on 29-30 September. Tradition is dear to the Pueblo. Bread is still baked in domed outdoor ovens. We visit some curio shops selling handcrafted wares—mica-flecked pottery, silver and turquoise jewellery, and tanned buckskin moccasins and drums. No wonder the early Spanish conquistadors believed that the pueblo was one of the fabled golden cities of Cibola.

After a quick visit to the Harwood Library—we pass a Hanuman Temple on the way—and an early dinner with Bob and Caroline, followed by a musical soirée at Mabel Luhan's Taos Estate, I am ready for bed. Next morning, I head out of Taos in a limo with the same driver who had driven me into Taos. "Did you have fun?" he asks. As I give him the thumbs-up sign, I recall what Lawrence wrote of this place: "New Mexico is the greatest experience I had from the outside world, it certainly changed me forever."

A Literary Treasure House: Humanities Research Centre, Texas, Austin, USA

The library at Austin, Texas, is a unique storehouse of priceless manuscripts, and rivals the ancient library at Alexandria.

The building that houses the Harry Ransom Humanities Research Center (HRC) in Austin, Texas, would not win any awards for high art. Not even the solitary fountain spouting water in a corner, as the only concession to beauty, can break the dull monotony of steel and concrete. Entry is restricted. It is impossible to proceed beyond the lobby without proper accreditation and prior permission. Inside, strapping six foot tall Texan security guards monitor the movement of visitors with the help of walkie-talkies, close-circuit video cameras, and high-tech alarm systems. No one is let out without a mandatory clearance slip.

The building's heavy security appears ill suited to the customary informality of an academic center, but there is clearly a good reason behind it. The HRC, which straddles Guadeloupe Street on the University of Texas campus, contains one of the world's most comprehensive and priceless collections of manuscripts, documents, and assorted memorabilia related to twentieth-century Western literature—primarily British, French and American. The center also has important collections in photography, film, theater arts, history of science, history of architecture, and books on arts and literary iconography.

The HRC is the dream of every lover of literature. Such a dream came my way in the Fall of 1990-91 when I won a Fulbright Post-Doctoral Fellowship to the United States to pursue my interest in the cultural history of the American Southwest. Soon after my arrival in Austin, the capital of Texas, my faculty associate Charles Rossman, and HRC Director Tom Staley, a distinguished James Joyce scholar, offered me an office space right inside the HRC building. This was a rare privilege, as I was soon to discover.

As one steps into this literary wonderland, a latter-day equivalent to the library of Alexandria, one falls under the magic spell of its prized holdings and exhibits. The main manuscript reading room on the fifth floor boasts the works, notes and scribblings primarily of twentieth-century poets, writers and artists—scratch books, diaries, memoirs, journals, workbooks, manuscripts, typescripts, first editions, correspondence of all sorts, special signed copies, etc.

The holdings have come from such twentieth-century giants as Dylan Thomas, G.B. Shaw, D.H. Lawrence, Samuel Beckett, Ezra Pound, James Joyce, Katherine Mansfield, Graham Greene, Saul Bellow, and Ernest Hemingway, as well as from many of their predecessors, among them Charles-Pierre Baudelaire, Robert Browning, Lewis Carroll, Lord Byron, and William Jones. The almost endless list of items in the collection blurs traditional distinctions between the "classics" and so-called popular or "low" literature.

These precious literary items, so painstakingly collected and carefully preserved with the help of modern technology, provide valuable clues to understanding culture and society—past, present, and future. They offer invaluable assistance to biographers as well as to cultural and literary critics. Notes and comments, carefully or casually left behind by poets and writers on successive versions of manuscripts, help us to understand the artistic process and to assess what Wordsworth described as the "growth of the poet's mind."

Over lunch one day at the faculty cafeteria, Warren Roberts, distinguished academic and one of the early directors of the HRC, explained how the University of Texas Chancellor Harry

Ransom established the Humanities Research Center in the late 1950s. Special university collections such as the Latin American Library and the Old Rare Books Collection were rapidly upgraded, and special emphasis was placed on acquiring more material pertaining to the twentieth century, an area in which the university already excelled.

Early builders of the HRC such as Ransom and Roberts relied on the holdings of private collectors, the archives of writers, the contents of bookstores, and the files of publishers and agents. The university had sufficient money to negotiate deals directly with collectors. Literary estates occasionally donated their holdings.

The experience of the HRC with private collectors offers a fascinating and rare glimpse into the sociology and folklore of the world of books and scholarship. Private collectors often concentrated in areas considered too archaic or arcane or avant-garde by institutional collectors. Some of these private collections, Roberts said, are now legendary. They include the Lee Samuel's Hemingway Collection, the Jerome Zipkin Collection of Somerset Maugham, the George Lazarus Collection of H.G. Wells and Arthur Rackham (English illustrator of children's books), and finally, the Ellery Queen Collection of detective fiction. Perhaps the most extraordinary contribution is by T.E. Hanley of Bradford, Pennsylvania. Hanley was no scholar in the traditional sense. However, he amassed an impressive range of material by Beckett, Lawrence and Shaw, long before the first two became celebrities. More than 2,200 pages exist in Lawrence's own handwriting for five of his leading works. These were supplemented later by materials and memorabilia acquired from his friends and acquaintances such as Dorothy Brett, Earl and Achsah Brewster, Knud Merrild, Helen Corke, and Edward McDonald. Similarly, the G.B. Shaw Collection contains most of his major plays in manuscript form and about 3,000 letters. Beckett's *Waiting for Godot* is preserved in a 163-page manuscript in English as well as a French version of 150 pages in Beckett's own handwriting.

Over the years, many authors or their estates sold or donated their archives to the HRC. Among them were Edgar Lee Masters, Christopher Morley, Maxwell Anderson, Paul Bowles, Louis Zukofsky, Tennessee Williams, and Evelyn Waugh.

As I walked through the glass-panelled reading room, listening to the quiet footfall of my feet, I would become mesmerised by this wonderland of literary treasures. I often thought that a library like the HRC, heir to such a priceless lore, certainly merited what the critic Walter Benjamin described as the "aura" or special cultic potency of all creative art work.

It was exhilarating to be able to examine and marvel at the copy of *The Waste Land* that T.S. Eliot prepared for the London Library Sale in 1960—it contains an extra line that did not appear in the printed version; or to stare at the holograph manuscripts of E.M. Forster's *Passage to India*, Aldous Huxley's *Brave New World*, O'Neill's *Mourning Becomes Electra*, Faulkner's *Absalom, Absalom*, and James Joyce's *Ulysses*, extensively corrected by the novelist; or to make the startling discovery of the first edition (1956) of a translation of Eliot's *Waste Land and Other Poems* by poet Gyanendra Varma into Oriya with a special prefatory message by Eliot himself.

Approximately 2,450 scholars seek permission to use HRC's facilities each year. A faculty committee reviews and approves their requests. Scholars have full access to most documents. Restrictions have been placed on a few items at the request of their donors (sometimes for a certain number of years). Only pencils and notepaper are allowed inside the reading room. Documents can be removed only one at a time from specially air-conditioned vaults. Scholars are given special instruction on how to handle them. Photo duplication, for which permission from the copyright holders is required, is generally discouraged because it tends to shorten the life span of the already-brittle manuscripts.

I thoroughly enjoyed my time at the HRC. Several images linger in my mind—the weekly tea at which scholars could argue over obscure textual problems; enthralling talks by literary biographers like Jeffrey Mayers, who unveiled Joseph Conrad's torrid affair with American aviator-journalist Jane Anderson; the weekly British Studies seminars where, over white wine or sherry, one can hear someone like Asian Studies expert Robert King explain the mission of William Jones in nineteenth-century India; the Christmas Eve literary bash where Austin academics reveal their lists of the best and the worst readings of the year; and exhibits of, among other items, a 1455 Gutenberg Bible, photographs and curios. . . .

The importance of a place like the HRC lies in recognising the crucial role that literature plays in society. For literature, as Harry Levin said, is not only "the most expressive source of documentation, but also the final residue of historical process." There could not be a more apt description of the Humanities Research Center at Austin.

Subverting Hegemonic Histories: Cairo, Egypt

An interesting account of the international symposium on "History in Literature" held in Cairo. Distinguished scholars like Edward Said and others from Asia, Africa, Australia, Europe and America, not to mention many from Egypt, attended the historic literary meet.

St. George's Hotel, Cairo. It's Christmas season and I have Santa's glorious options—a cruise on the Nile, a visit to the Pyramids, or a talk by the very distinguished Edward Said of Columbia University. The international symposium on *History in Literature* is on with scholars from Asia, Africa, Australia, Europe and the Americas, not to mention plenty from Egypt, the host country.

I glance at the schedule. It is good that Edward Said is strategically placed as the keynote speaker between the first and concluding day of the conference. We listen with rapt attention to the inaugural address by Gamal El Ghitany, one of Egypt's most notable and illustrious novelists. Ghitany's reflections on the many roots and traditions of the narrative in Egypt, from the Arabian Nights Entertainment to the prose of the Sufi mystics such as those of Abu Havyan and Ibu Arabi and epics and folk material incorporated in the written language are illuminating indeed! Ghitany tells us that the 1967 Arab-Israeli War, in its effect on him "was not only a significant moment in my personal history but also in the history of my nation." This made the novelist turn to Egypt's historical past, to moments of national humiliation such as the one Egypt suffered at the hands of the Turks in the nineteenth century.

It is appropriate that the issue Ghitany foregrounds are soon taken up by scholars who explore the fascinating interface between History and Literature. Loubna Youssef of Cairo University recounts the "History in the Ballads of British War Poets in the Western Desert in World War II," Daniel Vitkus of American University says Cairo offers a polemic on "History, Anachronism and Islam in the Drama of Christopher Marlowe."

Sandra Richards from Oxford captivates the audience with her "Serpent of Old Nile English Actresses and the Challenge of Cleopatra." Comparative topics are plenty—"Crusades in Shakespeare's Histories," "Ancient Egypt and Poets of Ireland." And then there is an insightful paper by Christina Civantos of the University of California at Berkeley, "Images of the Orient in the Construction of the Argentine Nation." Whoever knew that a remote Latin American could have a North African/Arab connection as well! There is a conspicuous absence of scholars from the Far East, and I am the only one to hold up the banner from South Asia. At lunchtime at the faculty cafeteria, I am accosted by a group of Masters students who wish to know the history of Amitabh Bachchan, especially his marital status! Amitabh, I realise, is a craze in Egypt. His *Coolie* is an icon here. I make a note to decipher the reason once I am back home. Later, I run into Asmat Mehdi, fellow Hyderabadi and Director of the Indian Cultural Centre at Cairo. Everyone tells me that Dr. Mehdi has done excellent work in Egypt. There is a lot of goodwill for India, but not enough knowledge, I am afraid. I am asked to speak a sentence in "Indian." "Which one?" I ask a group of perplexed students. "There are sixteen officially recognised languages in India, not to mention English, of course!"

Determined to highlight "our" standpoints—democracy, secularism, free press and active scholarship-I procure a map of India for my presentation. I am put in a slot along with Hoda El Sadda of Cairo University, a respected Egyptian feminist. Together we offer the Third World women's perspective in literature. I talk of "feminist historiography in an Indian province" and Hoda reconsiders the "history of anti-colonialism and feminism in Egypt." I meet Nina, the granddaughter of Egypt's best-known feminist, Hodda Sarawi, after whom a street in Cairo has been named. Nina informs me of Gandhi's passage through Port Said and asks me about non-violence and feminism.

It was Edward Said who was undoubtedly the star of the conference. For someone who enjoys a formidable worldwide reputation as one of our best contemporary original thinkers, straddling many disciplines and discursive practices underlined in *Orientalism* and the recent *Culture and Imperialism*, Edward Said has made the greatest single contribution in exposing the Eurocentric bias of the Western knowledge systems (otherwise projected as "universal"). Said comes across as a remarkably gentle, firm, friendly and accessible person, welcoming constantly a spirit of dialogue. His language, as he speaks, is fresh and crisp, refreshingly free from self-conscious pedantry or pompous jargon. It avoids all circumlocution endemic of so much of literary theoretical writing today. His sense of humour is dignified, and at such moments, his expression becomes deadpan, barring the occasional glint in his eyes.

As an opening remark, he said that he had come prepared to speak on "History and Literature" rather than "History in Literature." Perhaps the confusion arose on account of the fact that both he and Hoda Gindi, Chairperson and his schoolmate at Cairo, had equally illegible handwriting! Both were ignorant of computers and there was philosophical potential in dwelling on the difference between "History in" and "History and!" We heard a version of the intellectual history of the West from Edward Said. Focusing on some of the seminal thinkers such as Hegel, Marx, Lukács, Foucault and Gramsci, Said underlined the main currents of Western literary history and culture. For, if in Lukács' "Studies in European Realism" and elsewhere, there is an inheritance of the Hegelian legacy and the awareness of narrative "Time," then in Antonio Gramsci, the Italian Marxist thinker, who was imprisoned by Mussolini, there is a crucial "geographical awareness." If in the French thinker, Michel Foucault, there is a sense of the prison-house of language, Gramsci's "geographical awareness" enables him to break out of the prison-house of power. Again, if the Hegelian style offers metahistories and grand narratives, then the Gramscian style is responsible for deconstructing and problematising identity. Indeed, suggested Said, this style generates much of the modern critical practice. It accentuates fractures and disjunctions rather than secure unified wholes that traditional narratives and cognitive systems do.

Of the modern theoreticians, British critic Raymond Williams, especially in his *Country and the City*, was astonishingly aware of geography's linkage with criticism. Logically, therefore, argued Said, we need to highlight the face of the many "dissenting traditions" of women, of coloured people, of culturally, ethnically and economically marginalised grouping, and of the modern nation states. Said replied that it was better to offer resistance to the bigger monolithic nation that had always usurped the State apparatus for its hegemonic role. Wise words indeed that were echoed by other discussants and panellists at the conference!

In the panel "History and Arts," for instance, Tarek Ali Hassan, former Director of the Egyptian National Cultural Centre, focused on the need to "question our Arab heritage, deconstruct our Arab history." He regretted that "forces have turned Egyptian society into a non-questioning society." Similarly, Nehad Selecha, talented drama critic, and Mahmud El Lozy, theatre activist from American University at Cairo, made a plea for the need to capture the Arab folk heritage that is always pluralistic. "We must not offer a blind submission to inherent readings of history," they said. For what is illegitimate art if not art close to the power centres!

As the conference got over, it was time to act on Santa's promise. Later, as we sat at the Mahufuz café, in the oriental bazaar of Cairo's Khan el Khalili, marvelled at the grand pyramids at Giza, took the cruise on the Nile, and strolled through the quaint historic quarters of Beit El Harawy (behind the Al Azhar mosque), we recalled the many questions and some answers that the Cairo conference on *History and Literature* had generated. As the German critic Walter Benjamin had rightly remarked: "There is no document of civilisation that is not at the same time a document of barbarism."

An Easterner in Eastwood–I: Nottinghamshire, UK, 1990

Winds of change may have swept across this quaint little town in the British Midlands, but the sights and sounds in the birthplace of D.H. Lawrence retain enough charm for the aficionado, as the author discovers.

It had rained the night before. I part the curtains from my upstairs room in the Hylands Hotel, close to Nottingham University, and look out. August 14 promises to bring clear skies and a hope of sunshine. It had better be a clear day, I decide. Having come halfway around the world (courtesy British Council and the Fulbright), I wasn't going to allow the proverbially bad English weather ruin my one-day trip to Eastwood.

The drive of eight-and-a-half miles from Nottingham to Eastwood is pleasant, but nothing tells you that this is D.H. Lawrence's fabled "country of my heart." You don't see "the red sandstone and the oak trees of Nottingham and the cold limestone, the ash trees, the stone fences of Derbyshire." As the motorway snakes forward, you spot, half a mile from Eastwood, signposts announcing "D.H. Lawrence's Birthplace." Obvious efforts of Broxtowe Borough Council, explains Julie Murdy, my escort.

And suddenly you are there. On the face of it, there is nothing distinct about this remote Midland town. You go down an incline and arrows everywhere point to your destination—the Birthplace Museum. Turning right, along Nottingham Road to Victoria Street, on the left, you find Number 8A, the birthplace of D.H. Lawrence. As our car pulls up near "Phoenix Craft Centre" and "Chatterley Art Gallery," we run into Joan McCluskey, the secre ary of the museum. My escorts take leave and I step inside 8A, Victoria Street.

I am welcomed by Rosemary Howard, the editor of the *Lawrence Newsletter*. She has not been deterred by her obvious cold. Having just returned from Peter Preston's big conference on D.H.L. at Montpellier in France, she is full of news. I feel I am in the company of my "family!"

The museum itself is admirably kept, with period furniture, many items dating back to Lawrence's time. Upstairs, you watch a video film of D.H.L's early life in Eastwood and take a tour of the museum. When you spend years with an author, he becomes a part of you. Every small place frequented by him, every line written by him, and every item he handled becomes for you an object of wonder. Now that you're taking a walk back into history, you're in a sentimental mood. Can something be done about a picture, I wonder. Someone sends for "George." George turns out to be, not a professional photographer, but George Hardy, an old Eastwood hand, co-author of the popular "D.H. Lawrence Album," a collection of rare photographs dating back to Lawrence's times. Like Rosemary, George too is almost down with flu, but he obliges me with pictures, and thoughtfully autographs a copy of his book I buy.

Together with Joan and Rosemary, I step out from 8A, Victoria Street. The road slopes down and you get a truly majestic view of Brinsley and Underwood. Too bad the collieries have been shut down. You content yourself with history alone. My escorts point out the building that once housed the offices of Barber, Walker and Co., the Colliery Company (Carson, Waite and Co. of Lawrence's autobiographical novel *Sons and Lovers*). We quickly visit 28 Garden Road, the end-house of what was at one time a colliery tenement block where the Lawrences moved from Victoria Street, and later to 8 Walker Street, where they moved again in 1891.

By now, it's noon. Time for Rosemary to return to Nottingham. Why not go to *White Peacock Café*, I suggest to my guides.

Why the name *White Peacock* for a café, I ask the lively proprietress at the counter. "Well, *White Peacock* is the first novel Lawrence wrote." And as an afterthought she adds, "We couldn't have named it after *Lady Chatterley*, you know; might have kept decent folks away!" As we savour the fresh coffee and German cakes, Rosemary points out that unfortunately, despite commerce, a lot of prejudice regarding Lawrence still remains in this hamlet.

We bid goodbye to Rosemary, and Joan offers to let me have a close look at the Eastwood countryside. We spot the Moorgreen Reservoir in the distance, but unfortunately cannot get any closer. I learn that the Barber family lives there. During Lawrence's days, they held a party there every Whit Monday. The drowning tragedy of the Crich in Lawrence's outstanding novel *Women in Love* was based on an actual fatality, and the Barber family till today has not taken too kindly to Lawrence for having "used" their family tragedy. Consequently, Lawrence admirers are welcome here like pests. We respect the dead and drive past The Haggs Farm of the [Jessie] Chambers family. As Lawrence's childhood sweetheart, Jessie was the model for Miriam of *Sons and Lovers*. Later, we stop at the Brinsley Colliery, which was the setting for *Odour of Chrysanthemums*, another haunting tale of Lawrence based on his mother's experience; the sudden death of a miner becomes paradoxically a means of escape for the entrapped wife in the claustrophobic village. The cottage that Lawrence portrayed in the story is in a state of disrepair. We talk to the owner of the building who lazily asks me if I would contact the Lawrence Society in America when I reach Texas. I promise to do what I can. Joan is not impressed: "The man dishes out the same excuse every time," she tells me. "Why can't he, instead, add a little plaster to chipped brickwork," she wonders.

A little drive and we reach the home of Margaret Needham, Lawrence's niece and one of the few surviving members of the immediate family. Peggy is ninety, but irrepressibly chirpy about her famous Uncle Brit, as she offers tea and chocolate cake. I buy an audio cassette of Peggy's reminiscences. We thank her and leave.

By now, it's sundown. Back in Eastwood, as our car goes around a bend, I spot, suddenly, near Victoria Street "E.T. Cut-piece Centre." I recall that E.T. was the penname Jessie Chambers used when she published her memoir "D.H. Lawrence: A Personal Record." Could it be named after Jessie Chambers, I wonder. It is there in Eastwood! How much of it is a belated tribute to a maligned local genius and how much due to commerce and tourism, Lawrence's "bitch-goodness," it's hard to tell. But either way, one is impressed with Broxtowe Borough Council. The local library it runs holds a special section devoted to Lawrence.

It's late evening when Joan drops me off at the Hylands Hotel. I thank the weather and sit down to ruminate over a day filled with lasting impressions.

An Easterner in Eastwood–II: Nottinghamshire, UK, 1999

Returning to Eastwood after a gap of eight years, I follow the newly laid "Blue Line Trail." I trace D.H. Lawrence's footsteps in "the country of my heart," and explore the landscape and the people of this unique town of the British Midlands that shaped Lawrence's career and personality.

If you are in those parts again, go to Eastwood where I was born and lived for my first 21 years. Go to Walker Street, stand in front of the third house and look across the Crich on the left. Underwood in front—High Park Woods and Annesley on the right, I lived in that house from the age of six to eighteen and I know that view better than anyone in the world . . . that is the country of my heart . . .

D.H. Lawrence in a letter to Rolf Gardiner from Italy in 1926

19 July 1999:

The newly introduced coach of "The Rainbow Bus Service" pulls up at the Victoria Bus Station, next to Nottingham City Centre. I look skyward with anxiety before getting in. Mercifully, it is a cloudy day, but not threateningly dark. Eight miles and forty minutes later at MI (Motorway) Junction 26, we turn inward. The first stop is the Eastwood Public Library at Wellington Place, the promised rendezvous with my local escort. I get off, and Fred Skillongton, local co-ordinator of the D.H. Lawrence Society, greets me warmly, "Welcome to Eastwood!"

he says enthusiastically. Two days earlier, I had met Fred at a meeting of the Society at Nottingham, courtesy Rosemary Howard, editor of The D.H. Lawrence Society, Nottingham.

While the habitat of every writer has a unique significance for an aficionado, nothing, I know, can rival D.H. Lawrence's relationship with Eastwood. It passed through various phases in his career—the uncritical acceptance of childhood, the sceptical rejection of manhood, and the nostalgia of middle ages. Despite all his international experience, it must be said that DHL remained, till the very end, a quintessentially English novelist. "For me as a young boy," he wrote of his early experience at Eastwood, "it was still the old England of the forest and the agricultural past, there were no motor cars, the mines were in a sense an accident, and Robin Hood and his merry men were not far away."

Eastwood was thus more than a "spirit of place" to Lawrence; it was integral to his narrative vision. It became "Bestwood" in *Sons and Lovers*, "Beldover" in *Aaron's Rod* and *Women in Love*, "Woodhouse" in *The Lost Girl*, and "Eberwich" in *The White Peacock*. Similarly, it is believed that the "village of Tevershall" in *Lady Chatterley's Lover* may have been modelled after Eastwood. The novel dates back to his final days and might suggest a return to his early moorings after his experience in Italy, Sri Lanka, Australia and the New World. The love-hate relationship that DHL shared with his birthplace is evocatively captured in an essay called "Return to Bestwood," which he wrote when he made a return trip at the age of forty-one.

The most remarkable thing that strikes a visitor who was returning to Eastwood after eight years, as I did, is the extent of changes visible. During his lifetime, Lawrence was not exactly a favourite local lad. His notoriety and ill fame as a writer of "dirty novels" was particularly felt in his hometown. Today, however, he is institutionalised and is an official icon. How much of it is genuine admiration and how much on account of tourism and money, Lawrence's bitch goddess, it is hard to surmise. However, there is plenty of evidence of the latter, as I soon discover.

At the entrance to the town, the road is flanked by rows of phoenix designs fixed against the brass railings, DHL's emblem of the mythical bird rising from its ashes, a symbol of life eternal. The library is soon going to install a phoenix, for which plans are underway. At the entrance to the library, you see a stone monument in high relief that depicts a Lawrentian couple in a state of close embrace. Below the statue, there are carvings of men at the labyrinthine, subterranean world, digging under the pitheads. A fitting homage indeed to the novelist and his habitat.

At Eastwood, the most remarkable change obviously is the "Blue Line Trail" on the pavement. It is the first such line in the country based upon the famous "Heritage Trail" in Boston, United States. The Department of Transport, one learns, has given special approval for the use of the blue line that links the DHL birthplace museum, The Heritage Centre, with three other houses he lived in and eight Lawrence-related sites.

We drive along the "Blue Line." Our first stop is the Eastwood Cemetery at the junction between Chewton Street and Main Street. We pass through the grave of William Hopkin, DHL's friend and mentor, and a local celebrity, and reach Lawrence's family grave, recently renovated. We bow in salutation to the memory of the departed. There is a bouquet of flowers inviting attention to the tombstone.

We emerge from the cemetery. On Mill Road, opposite Beauvale Methodist Church, we stand before the "D.H. Lawrence Infants School" (named after the novelist) maintained by Nottinghamshire County Council. DHL was a pupil here in 1898. We visit the school and are cordially taken around by the headmistress Mrs. Pam. Brenda, a volunteer teacher whose grandfather went to the same school with DHL, and two lovely children deputed by Mrs. Pam, Joshua and Alexandra. We visit DHL's old schoolroom and recall his words regarding the learning of the young. We also recall his hauntingly beautiful animal poems. The school itself is a series of red brick Gothic-style buildings with turrets and high gabled roofs.

We retrace our steps. Close to Church Street at New Eastwood, Fred points out a house that he says is the site where stood a dwelling depicted in DHL's novel, *Mr. Noon*. "You must read about the character, Amy Bostock," suggests Fred knowledgeably. We are greeted by Stan and Joan Bradley, owners of the current house, somewhat ornate. It is amazing how much of Eastwood's landscape went into DHL's fiction.

We drive up to Lynncroft Street. The fourth DHL family house exists here; this is where Mrs. Lydia Lawrence died in 1910, alas, before the publication of DHL's first novel. The house had a garden with a field at the back. While living here, DHL worked as a pupil teacher at the British School in Albert Street and trained at Ilkeston. Later, he qualified himself at Nottingham University and left Eastwood for a post at Croyden in 1908.

From Lynncroft Street, you have a lovely view of DHL's "country of my heart"—the Toneygrey Farm, and beyond, Brinsley village. Here you meet a block of houses where DHL lived from 1891 to 1902. These buildings enjoy an elevated position and offer a majestic view north across to the countryside. From here, Fred explains, DHL continued his education at the Beauvale Public School, travelled for three years to Nottingham Boys High School, and spent a short time working at a Surgical Appliance Factory in Nottingham's Lace Market.

Follow the "Blue Line Trail" and come next to Walker Street. The Lawrence family moved into a house here in 1897. It was better than the place on 8 Victoria Street. It has a scullery and a small porch. Most important of all, it was an end house and therefore had a large private garden. Blocks of houses contained the ash pits that provided "a communal area where children played, women gossiped, and men smoked."

From Walker Street, we drive up to the Durban House, renovated in 1998. Initially built in 1876 as the office of Barber Walker and Company, the major coal owner in Eastwood and the surrounding area, the building was also used as an official institute for social activities including a billiard room and a ballroom.

We recall the scene in *Sons and Lovers* where Paul Morel goes to the head office to collect his father's wages. After nationalisation of coal, the structure was converted into flats for national coal board employees brought from other regions to work in the mines.

We pay the admission fee and enter the sparklingly renovated Durban House, so named after the South African connection of the owners, the Barber family. In one of the most imaginative moves that seeks to combine an interest in the preservation of local culture with an eye for tourism, the Broxtowe Borough Council has created a marvel with local, national and European funding. Today, the Durban House Heritage Centre is a complex that houses a shop, a restaurant, and other facilities in the ground floor. Upstairs, we are captivated by an audio-visual spectacle comprising life-size photographs and background voice that record DHL's upbringing and career in Eastwood. The highlight clearly is a scene from *Sons and Lovers*, where Paul and Miriam (DHL and Jessie Chambers) are depicted reading to each other at the Hags Farm. Part of the exhibition also captures the period history, especially the life of the miners that has an interface with DHL's own biography. Apt quotations from DHL's essays like "Nottingham and the Mining Countryside" lend literary authenticity to a bygone cultural era of the British Midlands.

By now, it has begun to drizzle. We pick up souvenir items, have coffee and sandwiches, and turn to 8 Victoria Street, DHL's birthplace. Complementary to the Heritage Centre, the Museum offers a time capsule of Victorian life. It records the home life of Mrs. Arthur Lawrence and her growing family. Upstairs, there is more of period costume and furniture. A video tells you of DHL's indebtedness to Eastwood.

As the sky begins to darken, Fred drives me quickly through Colliers Wood and the Brinsley Colliery. At the latter site, plans are underway to reclaim the area as a picnic centre, a heritage and a conservative site. We stop by the Moorgreen reservoir. Constructed at the end of the eighteenth century to supply water to the Nottingham canal, the reservoir still retains its pristine charm and serenity. We recall the memorable scenes of Nethermere (in *The White Peacock*) and Willey Water (in *Women in Love*).

It is well past noon when we return to Eastwood. Fred bids me farewell at the library, and I return to Nottingham to ruminate over a day full of lasting impressions.

A Crop of Writers at Cambridge, UK

The Cambridge Seminar on the Contemporary British Writer, an institution that celebrated its twenty-fifth anniversary in July 1999, brought together acclaimed British writers. There were specialists from thirty-five countries of the English-speaking world. I was one of the five delegates from India.

As seminars go, it was a dream come true. It was hard to think of a better mix of writers, critics and translators, or of a better venue. There were some of the top writers of Britain—David Lodge, Malcolm Bradbury and George Steiner, Salman Rushdie, Harold Pinter and Doris Lessing. The new crop of writers was well represented too—Simon Armitage, Claire Tomalin, Andrea Levy, Michele Roberts and Penelope Lively.

There was a panel of translators to debate the issues—Eva Hoffman, Rukshana Ahmed and George Szirtes. And there was the most fitting locale—Downing College on Regent Street, of Cambridge University, the legendary home of F.R. Leavis. Above all, there was the liveliest group of Fellows from thirty-five nations—Australia, Azerbaijan, Canada, Croatia, India, Ireland, Pakistan, Portugal, Spain, Sweden, Ukraine, the United States, Zimbabwe . . . . The seminar was managed by Christopher Bigsby and Damian Grant, veterans in the field, under the overall leadership of Alastair Niven, Director of Literature at the British Council and a strong believer in the multicultural cause in English Studies. Nor was the seminar confined to only readings and deliberations.

There was a visit to "Antony and Cleopatra" at the Royal Shakespeare Company at Stratford-upon-Avon. There was also a tribute to Ted Hughes and Iris Murdoch, a walking tour of Cambridge, a Silver Jubilee dinner at the Sheen Mill restaurant, and a reception at the Heffers bookshop.

The Link between Biography and Literature

The seminar at Howard Hall (7-16 July 1999) opened with a discussion on the interesting, and at times vexing relationship between biography and literature. Michael Frayn and Claire Tomalin, eminent biographers, debated the related issues of truth and fiction, and science and sexuality in the mode of biography and autobiography. Frayn, whose recently published play "Copenhagen" was based on the life of the eminent physicist Heisenberg, said that plays could be as much about characters as opposed to plays that have a definite ideological agenda. Science is largely carried out through conversation. Heisenberg seems to accept this insight and therefore employs the mode of conversation in his memoir. In fact, Frayn maintained, fiction is the "paradigm case of scientific theory." On the other hand, biographies often unravel disturbing aspects of a subject's life, such as Wittgenstein's companionship with a man at Cambridge, or the aspect of sexuality in the life of Catherine Mansfield. Interesting questions followed—Did the biographer write against the fact of death in order to get rid of the subject?

A participant from India wanted to know why Indians produced hagiographies most of the time. And what was the culture's self-view of itself based on the realisation that it could not produce biographies? Frayn thought that the biographical mode was handled quite well by Indian writers. For instance, V.S. Naipaul's *The House for Mr. Biswas*, he thought, certainly offered an admirable fictional account of his father.

Salman Rushdie, credited with "The Intifada of the Imagination" by Edward Said, read out extracts. What was the relationship between novelist and screenplay writer?

Rushdie contended that an excessive respect for the author could be a constraint, referring to his own experience as a screenplay writer. There was the need to change the plot to suit the dramatic mode of the screenplay. Talking about his political novel, he revealed that *Shame*, unlike the popular view, was the "most directly political novel." Was cosmopolitanism a crime?, Rushdie asked rhetorically. Perhaps only in the eyes of late Marxist ideology and critics like Aijaz Ahmed, he retorted. His own work had been shaped by the experience of the city. It was this "metropolitan sensibility" that lent uniqueness to his art. Unfortunately, the declining interest in stories happened after modernism. Did Rushdie's art exemplify rootless liberation or a tragic predicament? Both, said Rushdie. After all, one should not forget that the novel arose along with the rise of the Nation State. Rootlessness was increasingly a contemporary experience. The idea of multiple belonging was a fact of life.

How did he look at the *Vintage Book of Indian Writing*, the commissioned work he undertook on the occasion of the fiftieth anniversary? I asked him the question that has troubled so many Indians—was Rushdie not being deliberately ignorant or dismissive about the rich world of regional literature in India? Rushdie stood his old ground and sounded quite unrepentant, although he did concede that regional writing in India was certainly more vibrant than what was evident in his anthology. On the other hand, he insisted that not many good works existed in translation. And in any case, the most significant thing that had happened in India in the last fifty years was the creation of Indian English literature.

A voice from Wales, the bilingual writer M.A. Humphreys, maintained that he was a non-cosmopolitan writer unlike Rushdie. Did he agree with Subaltern historian Deepesh Chakraborty that we could use the English language to reprovincialise Europe? Humphreys shared his experience as a bilingual writer working under the direct shadow of English. "By being bilingual," he said, "we create a war with ourselves." The word "Britain" comes from the word "Brutus." After all, claimed

Humphreys, the original inhabitants of Britain were the Welsh people. Thus, in a way, to go back to Chakraborty, the tension between languages could be creatively fruitful.

The readings by Simon Armitage, a poet of the new generation, revealed a remarkable dexterity with language and word play, a skill that he put to deadly use in his BBC travel and tourism documentaries.

Poetry was well matched by fiction. David Lodge, one of the better known of the English novelists who has written international fiction, primarily for his "academic novels," read out extracts from his soon-to-be-published novel. The extract, which captured an encounter between the interviewer and the interviewee in a typical English country house, had all the elements of vintage Lodge—humor, sexual parody, and above all, the frisson characteristic of an interview situation where the partners belonged to the opposite sex. All these showed Lodge's success in having captured public imagination. Attention was also drawn to lesser-known aspects of Lodge's career—as a dramatist, a screenplay writer, and as the Chairman of the jury for the Booker Prize.

The line-up of celebrities continued with Andrew Motion, Poet Laureate of Britain. Although he did write and was required to write "public poems," Motion said he "hates poems that have a palpable design on us." Poetry he regarded as a part of national conversation. It was hard to find a true voice that addressed the whole of Britain, he admitted. He therefore strongly felt "English" rather than "Scottish." He preferred to write personal poems, and used simple language. Personal suffering, physical illness, and the death of his mother were the genesis of many of his personal poems.

Did the institution of the poet laureateship by the State deradicalise the poet? He conceded with remarkable candor that there was always that danger. Motion, a biographer, has published a life of Keats, and his model remains that of Tennyson, a poet speaking to fellow men.

Michele Roberts, who is half French, read out extracts from her book, where scholars from the monastery crave the whores in the underground bordello, while the whores manifest a powerful desire for books even as they minister to the needs of the male scholars every night. They run upstairs whenever they possibly can. In this interesting reversal of gender stereotypes promoted by all cultures (i.e., male = intellect, female = passion), Roberts was making an important point regarding the making of civilisation. Her writing, she said, addressed the feminine-female question and attempted a balance between the abstract and the concrete. Her characters seemed to hover over gender. She spoke about the place of religion in her early upbringing as a Catholic. Describing herself as a heretic rather than a Catholic, she maintained, perhaps following D.H. Lawrence, that the Church was the fitting locale for sensuality. Thus, her writings explored the relationship between religion and sexuality.

The Expatriate Experience

There were two British writers at the conference who had a significant expatriate experience. One of them was Penelope Lively, who had an Egyptian background (till the age of twelve). In her novels, she has explored the boundaries of possibility in fiction, just as in her autobiography, of the notion of the "English" and the other.

The other important writer was Doris Lessing. Born in Iran, Lessing often brought in significant aspects of recent history, for instance, moulding the experience of World War II for her novelistic purpose.

Readings by Harold Pinter

The highlight of the seminar was the readings by Harold Pinter. Just as *Waiting for Godot*, a play discussed by avant-garde critics as incomprehensible, paradoxically captured an audience of hardcore inmates of the prison of San Quentin, Pinter's *The Birthday Party*, Bigsby said, recollecting his South

American experience, had a political resonance even in faraway Brazil. The *Comedy of Menace* that Pinter himself was famous for, was amply demonstrated in his own reading, perhaps not surprising because Pinter is a one-time actor. A strong opponent of the NATO (North Atlantic Treaty Organisation) bombing of Kosovo, Pinter acknowledged that his plays were certainly political. Although they were rooted in the British context, they had universal resonances.

The experience of colour was well illustrated in the work of Andrea Levy, a writer of Afro-Caribbean origin. Her *Pot*, which captured the bittersweet experience of an immigrant's arrival from Jamaica, was commissioned by the South Bank Theatre.

W.G. Sebald offered the perspective of a German writer in Britain. There was poetry reading by Fleur Adcock and Janice Galloway; a presentation by the celebrated Malcolm Bradbury who referred to the recent publication of the CIA (Central Intelligence Agency)-supported academic/ literary activity at the height of the Cold War; readings by Ferdinand Dennis; and an excellent lecture on the troubling theme "The Disappearance of Theatre" by Max Stafford Clark. In addition, there was a premier reading of a new play by Biyi Bandele called *Happy Birthday Mister Deka D*, which evoked a lot of interest in the work of the African playwright.

Extremely enjoyable were Ruth Rosen's beautiful readings from the works of Ted Hughes and Iris Murdoch, both of whom recently passed away. Equally delightful was the reception given by Heffers bookshop, which also displayed a set of books by the various speakers of the Cambridge meet. Most enjoyable of all were the readings of the Fellows themselves, who brought in an amazing range of literary cultural experiences.

The grand finale was undoubtedly offered by George Steiner. In his epic sweep of many disciplines, systems of thought and continents, Steiner offered a futuristic vision of literature in the age of biological clones and digital computers. If his vision appeared somewhat bleak, it was redeemed by the seminal place Steiner gave to humanism in his view of life and literature.

Final Impressions

So, what were my final impressions of the Cambridge seminar? It was a real privilege to be in the company of so many talented writers; to have the opportunity to carry out free, frank and long discussions.

I realised, however, that despite the best efforts of the organisers, the seminar often became Eurocentric in focus. To some extent, this was perhaps unavoidable. A large chunk of participation, after all, came from the former East-European bloc. The European Union was also committed to their cause. Sadly, the vast continent of Africa went unrepresented. Budgetary constraints were undoubtedly the greatest hurdle.

In addition, I had the uneasy feeling that at least some of the delegates from the non-European countries were unabashed Anglophiles, who unfortunately did not bring any vision to the collective deliberation, barring their uncritical admiration of all things Anglo-American.

As the closing day approached, and my eyes were riveted on the doorway of F.R. Leavis, I reflected on the strengths and weaknesses of the British literary-cultural tradition. I cast a glance in the direction of King's College, Cambridge, where, a century earlier, mystic, philosopher and poet Sri Aurobindo did his tripos and discarded the lure of the Indian Civil Service despite his success in the examinations.

It was then that the lesson of the example set by perhaps the greatest sage/philosopher of our country came to me with renewed force—in our cultural travel to the West, I realised that even as we marvel, we must always learn to match our new learning with the wisdom of our own traditions and heritage.

Small is Always Beautiful: The Writers' Workshop Story

The Writers' Workshop has a unique position in the Indian literary and publishing world. Its pivotal role is to define and substantiate the creative role of English by discussion and diffusion of creative writing from India and other parts of the world. Here, the author profiles the man behind the institution.

Why should Sheaffer Inc., Rhode Island, U.S.A., one of the largest manufacturers of calligraphy products, support literary awards of a small publishing house in far away Calcutta? The question certainly is as fascinating as the history of the Writers' Workshop or its founder, Professor P. Lal. Over a period spanning 35 years, Lal, a one-man institution, has carved out for himself and his workshop a unique position in the Indian literary and publishing world.

The eagerness of Sheaffer to sponsor awards in the form of five 23-carat gold electroplated fountain pens, one each for the best book in five categories—poetry, drama, fiction, literary criticism, and *belles lettres*—is just one more instance. Lal believes that good work has never suffered due to lack of money or patronage. "Such work has to be genuine and selfless," he continues. It is this firm faith in the worthiness of creative effort that has always guided Lal. In a publishing world that is shockingly unprofessional and grossly mercenary, the sustained work of the Writers' Workshop has forced attention upon the sceptics, if only by its clear success over a period of time.

Finding the Writers' Workshop in Calcutta's sprawling Lake Gardens surprisingly poses no problem. Everybody seems to know "the Professor," I ring the bell and am ushered upstairs to Lal's bed-cum-study. Lal sits in a corner amidst a vast pile of books, wrapping paper, scissors, thread, gum bottles, and above all, a collection of strikingly attractive calligraphy pens. "This is the workshop," he explains. "I do practically everything myself, starting from correspondence to making neat parcels." Anyone who has worked with the WW knows that it is not an empty boast.

All correspondence with the Workshop, as many must have discovered, is invariably in Lal's own handwriting. Letters are promptly answered, schedules scrupulously kept. "I have just recovered from near death," Lal explains his pulled-down look. In 1989, while attending the "Harbour Front Poetry Reading Series" in Canada, Lal was suddenly taken ill. The recovery, he feels, was miraculous. "I have had so many bottles of blood transfusion that I am not sure if I am still a Hindu," he remarks with a laugh. The experience has weakened him, but certainly not his effort.

I ask Lal about the beginning. "The reason I went into publishing is simple," he says and goes on to add:

> Nobody was around in 1958 to publish me. So, I published myself. Half a dozen others—friends—also found this expedient, attractive. So we formed a group, a nice consanguineous coterie. We wrote prefaces to each other's books, pointing out excellences, and performed similar familial kindness in other ways as well. We believed with Helen Gardner that criticism should flash the torch, not wield the sceptre. We gave unto ourselves a name—Writers' Workshop-and adopted a detailed 1,000-word "constitution," drafted by our precise member, Deb Kumar Das.

Apart from Das, there were seven others—Sasthi Brata, Anita Desai, William Hull, P. Lal (as the secretary), Jai Ratan, Pradin Sen, and Kewlian Sio.

The objective of the WW has always centred around the pivotal role that English language can and ought to be playing creatively in India. English, it believes,

> has proved its ability as a language to play a creative role in Indian literature. The task the Workshop has set for itself is that of defining and substantiating this role by discussion and diffusion of creative writing from India and other parts of the world. Its publishing focuses on English, creative and transcreative works by Indians, or such works as deal with or are inspired by or have relevance to Indian life and culture.

Today, the WW has 800 titles on its list, mostly poetry, drama, fiction and criticism by mostly young and unknown Indian authors. Operating with a small band of devoted workers, with the total machinery including typefaces costing less than Rs.6,000, using vacant space thoughtfully provided by friends as godowns and storage, the WW has been able to keep down costs to a minimum, roughly one-fifth the cost of a Linotype press. The books are invariably hand-set and printed on an Indian-made hand-operated machine by Sanjoy Chakroborty. They are also gold-embossed, hand-stitched, hand-pasted, and hand-bound by Tulamiah Mohiudeen in handloom saree cloth.

What are the workshop's criteria for selection, I ask Lal. "It has three. One, a writer sends in material that's so impossibly good that it's a few years ahead of its time—and there are very few commercial publishers who would think of investing in such first rate post-dated creativity. Two, the work shows promise and the writer might stop writing altogether if not discreetly encouraged through publishing. Three, the manuscripts appeal to my taste, such as it is, and I enjoy bring out stuff that I like; it's like introducing a talented friend to strangers, though some may well wonder where the talent lies. To each his taste! A good motto to go by is: publish the moderns and read the ancients. Trust ruthless time."

The record of the WW has clearly been impressive. Several writers, who went on to bag important literary awards, made their debut here. The Workshop published Nissim Ezekiel's *The Unfinished Man* in 1960 and *The Exact Name* in 1965. Ezekiel went on to claim the Sahitya Akademi award in 1984. Similarly, none could have imagined Jayanta Mahapatra for the same award in 1981 when ten years before in 1971, his book of poems *Svayamvara* was published. Or that *Time* would feature Kamala Das in its 27 December 1975 issue, when her work *The Descendants* appeared in the WW in 1967. Or that Vikram Seth, whose collection of poems *Mappings* was brought out by WW in 1985 would be honoured with the Sahitya Akademi for his *Golden Gate* three years later. The Workshop also takes pride in being the first publishers of Ruskin Bond (in India), Asif Currimbhoy, Keki Daruwalla, Shashi Deshpande, Padma Hejmadi, Shiv K. Kumar, David McCutchion, Pritish Nandy, A.K. Ramanujan, Jai Ratan, Jug Suraiya, and many others who have subsequently distinguished themselves in large commercial houses.

The Workshop has received many coveted awards for its excellent production too. It won the first prize in the National Printing and Binding awards (1970) for William Hull's *Vision of Handy* (Hopper Books) and for Jai Nimbkar's *The Lotus Leaves*.

The activities of the WW are many and go beyond publishing new titles. A bi-monthly journal *Miscellany* serves as a forum for critical reviews. Sunday morning sessions are devoted to informal readings or discussion by scholars and creative writers. Over the years, the reputation of the Workshop has brought many distinguished writers to Lake Gardens—Mulk Raj Anand, Pearl S. Buck, Nirad C. Chaudhuri, Paul Engle, Allen Ginsberg, Gunther Grass, Geoffrey Hill, Christopher Isherwood, William Radice, R.K. Narayan, Raja Rao, Santha Rama Rao, Peter Brook, Jean Claude Carriere, Karan Singh, and many more.

How does P. Lal keep going? After all, even poets and small publishers need money. A modest subsidy from a writer may be asked for, but it may not offset the cost of production of a book, especially when several editions must remain unsold.

After all, few people buy books, and fewer still the work of a totally unknown author. Lal is quick to point out that a venture such as this is not a commercial proposition. Nevertheless, he has never relied on government support, keeping the WW scrupulously apolitical. He does not blame the commercial houses either. "They are primarily interested in money and so they must have their pot-boilers," he shrugs. "There is certainly space both for the banyan tree as well as the grass."

"Every year," he continues, "I get invited to lecture at North American universities. Most of the money I earn there goes into my books." Assignments from abroad also help. As if to prove this point, Lal pulls out an envelope and hands over a letter to me. A prestigious international agency wants him to make an assessment of creative writing in India in the last five years. The reward for a 500-word resume—$2000. "That's good money," says Lal. "Quality work is always recognised here and abroad, and international foundations prefer dealing with non-governmental organisations of repute in the Third World."

Lal's own achievements are by no means modest. He is honorary Professor of English at Calcutta University. From 1962, he has lectured widely on Indian literature to British, American and Australian universities such as the University of Illinois, Hofstra, Ohio, as well as Albion, Hartwick and Berea College. Transcreations from the epics and scriptures have been many—*The Dhammapada, The Isa Upanishad* (1947, 1967), *The Mahabharata* of Vyasa (1980), *The Ramayana* of Valmiki (1981). Current projects include *The Complete Mahabharata* of Vyasa. Lal is also the Director of the research and publication unit of the MP Birla Foundation, publishers of the 30-volume *Encyclopedia Asiana* and the 50-volume series *Classics of the East*. There has been recognition at the national level too—the prestigious Jawaharlal Nehru Fellowship in 1969-70, as well as Padma Shri in 1970.

Lal attributes much of his success to a happy marriage. A son and a daughter are both in the literary world. His wife, a creative person and a designer herself, continues to remain an active partner.

While there has been an occasional criticism that the WW has lent its imprint of the flame-ringed Bird book logo at times to undeserving titles, it goes to the Workshop's credit that it has so far steered clear of major controversies, preferring to turn out works quietly and efficiently. At 60-plus, when many may call it a day, Professor Lal and his Workshop have proved yet again that small is always beautiful!

The School That D.H. Lawrence Went To

Although hailed as a literary genius, D.H. Lawrence's views on education, particularly of the young, is little known. In this account based on a recent trip to Eastwood, Nottinghamshire, I profile the Greasley Beauvale School, renamed after the novelist and discuss the relevance of DHL's progressive ideas to our own schooling system in India.

Barring the exceptionally few who have the good fortune to go to schools such as the Sri Aurobindo International Centre at Pondicherry or Rishi Valley in the Chittoor District of Andhra Pradesh, most children unfortunately find schooling a form of tyranny and captivity, as did D.H. Lawrence in his birthplace Eastwood, towards the end of the nineteenth century. Although I have made several scholarly trips to Nottingham, it is only recently that I came across a significant aspect of the genius' upbringing at the "Greasley Beauvale D.H. Lawrence Infants' School." I believe this account is of relevance to our own milieu.

But before I tell you something about Lawrence's school, perhaps I ought to briefly give you an idea about the outstanding literary artist. D.H. Lawrence was born in 1885 in a coalminer's family. His father, Arthur Lawrence, worked at the local Brinsley coal pits. His mother, Lydia, had great aspirations for her children. Lawrence rose from the working class background and went on to become one of the most celebrated and prophetic writers of the twentieth century. He distinguished himself most of all in writing about the relationship between men and women. He died in Vence, France, in 1930, and his ashes were buried at

Taos, New Mexico, by his widow Frieda and companion Mabel Dodge Luhan.

There are, however, many aspects of Lawrence's writings that make a special appeal to children. In school, some of us may have read his hauntingly beautiful animal poems like "The Snake," "The Mosquito" and "The Bat." Clearly, we marvel at his uncanny habit of capturing the spirit of the animal world.

It was, thus, with special pleasure that I accompanied a local Lawrence enthusiast Fred Skillington, who doubled up as my guide in Eastwood in July 1999. We drove to Lynncroft on a sunny day to the Dovecote Road, and 350 yards on the left spotted the school Lawrence went to. It sported a signboard in bright red. The image of the Phoenix, Lawrence's emblem of the mythical bird that rose from its ashes, was strategically placed on the board. Lawrence was apparently the first pupil from this school (now named after him; then known as the Beauvale Board School) to win a scholarship to go to the Nottingham High School.

We stood outside the school and hesitated whether we should enter. "No harm in trying!" said Fred as he went in. He soon reappeared with a smile on his face. "You're lucky, Sachi," he beamed, "the headmistress would be happy to receive you!" Clearly, our fear was misplaced. The headmistress, Mrs. Pam, greeted us warmly. She escorted us to the Teachers' Room where I was introduced to all present. I exchanged notes and pleasantries with Brenda, a volunteer-teacher. Brenda had reasons for her special love with the institution; her grandfather went to school with D.H. Lawrence. It's amazing how cohesive the entire township of Eastwood could be. In between our conversation, the headmistress filled in relevant details about the school.

The land for the school, Pam began, was rented from Lord Cowper at a nominal price. The shape of the land is peculiar and required a plan of unusual character. Originally, the school housed three departments. The girls used the Dovecote Road Wing, the boys the Mill Road Wing, and the infants diagonally between the two. Originally, it was built for 55 children—200 boys, 200 girls, and 150 infants. Since 1976, the school had been used for infants only from four-and-a-half to seven years of age. Externally, the building is exactly as it was a hundred-and-eight years ago!

In 1976, the newly appointed Head of the Infants' School, with the help of the local CID, had two cast-iron safes opened. Inside were documents dating from the school's opening until the 1930s that had been locked away at that date and forgotten. George Hardy of the local history society searched the documents and found the signatures of several of the Lawrence children and a wealth of material currently housed in the Nottinghamshire Country Record Office. An examination of the Infants' School Admission Register for the years 1888-1900 shows that David Herbert Lawrence was initially a pupil at the school from 20 May 1889 to 20 October 1889. Later, he continued his education in the Boys' Department.

No sooner had Pam left us than two lovely children came forward to greet us. "Good morning, my name is Joshua!" said the boy. "Hello, I'm Alexandra!" piped in the little girl. "We've been asked by Mrs. Pam to show you around." "That would be fantastic!" I responded to the duo in their bright red tops that displayed the ubiquitous Lawrence emblem of the Phoenix.

It was a pleasure to be escorted by Joshua and Alexandra. We walked through the contemporary staff-parent lounge where there is a "picture quotations" collage, and went along a short corridor. This is where we came to the D.H. Lawrence Schoolroom. The original fireplace is preserved, but unfortunately is painted white instead of the original black lead. It is currently used as a Music Room. The gallery that was D.H. Lawrence's first seat of learning has long since been removed, but the marks on the wall show where it was once fixed.

Although Lawrence's memories of his schooling are relatively scanty, his views on the oppressive nature of the education of his day, a carryover of the Victorian era, are scattered throughout his writings. Alas, even today, we seem to follow such a pathetic and soul-killing system in our country. In fact, so appalled was DHL by this system that he gave up his career as an apprentice teacher.

A faith in an idealistic system of learning was a lifelong quest of Lawrence. At one time, he thought of locating such a utopia, a sort of commune called Rananim at Florida, a project that never took off. Practicality was never a virtue with the novelist!

However, Lawrence's adolescent characters are often shown to battle against the Dickinson educational system portrayed in *Hard Times*. For instance, his female protagonist, Ursula Brangwen in his celebrated *The Rainbow* is found to rebel as a young teacher against the inhuman and impersonal schooling system. He critiques and ridicules constantly the tyranny that masquerades as education. "We talk about education," he once remarked, as "leading forth the natural intelligence of a child. But ours is just the opposite of leading forth. It is a ramming in of brain, facts through the head, and a consequent distortion and starvation of the primary centres of consciousness."

Fortunately today, Lawrence's old school seems to be a living testimony to his own ideal as a centre that is vibrant, lively and joyous. The school has won many laurels. Its historical importance is generally acknowledged in the local country affairs and the media. Brenda often takes the children out to DHL's "country of my heart." Nearby are the colliers woods, the picturesque Moorgreen Reservoir, Vine Cottage, and Gossall Village—all immortalised in DHL's works. In one such outing, Pam informed us, when Brenda read out before the children Lawrence's essay "Adolf, the Rabbit," a real rabbit appeared from the undergrowth and charmed the children, who were lost in wonder.

It is not surprising that, of all things, it is the sense of wonder and creativity that was central to DHL's life and mission. "When all comes to all," he once observed, "the most precious element in life is wonder."

It was noon when we bid goodbye to Joshua, Alexandra, Brenda and Pam. We stood outside the school, a series of red brick Gothic-style buildings with turrets and high gabled roofs. As Fred and I retraced our footsteps, I recalled DHL's remark on education that would be music to the ears of children everywhere: "Don't set up standards and regulation patterns for people," he said prophetically. "Don't have criteria. Let every individual be single and self-expressive." One couldn't agree more!

The Future of Literature

George Steiner, one of the most gifted philosophers and cultural critics of post-war Europe, recently did some crystal ball gazing into the future of literature in an age of biological cloning, digital computers, and cyber narrations. His approach and allusions clearly go beyond the literary. His speech combines theoretical insights with down-to-earth documentation from the world of popular culture. He even mulls over the possibility of a truly global language. He spoke at the Cambridge Seminar in 1999 on the Contemporary British writer.

One of the most gifted and original philosophers and cultural critics of post-war Europe, George Steiner's international stature is matched only by the number of disciplines and intellectual systems he has come to master.

Born in Paris in 1929, George Steiner was educated at the Universities of Paris, Chicago, Harvard and Oxford. A winner of several coveted awards, including the Fulbright and Guggenheim, Steiner has been a Fellow at the Institute of Advanced Study, Princeton (1959-60).

He has been a Director of English Studies at Churchill College, Cambridge, and has been an "extraordinary" Fellow of the College since 1969. He was a Professor of English and Comparative Literature at the University of Geneva in 1974.

His publications include *In Bluebeard's Castle* (1971), *Proofs and Three Parables* (1975), *Antigones* (1984), *Proofs and Three Parables* (1992), *Errata* (1998), *Language and Silence: Essays on Language, Literature and the Human* (1998).

George Steiner belongs to an intellectual era that celebrated a wide-ranging versatility as the hallmark of true learning and wisdom.

Of medium height and impeccably dressed, Steiner's gestures and articulations have the same grace and lucidity that his prose is characteristic of; its straightforwardness and declamatory tone adequately mirror his futuristic vision of literature.

Although Steiner is widely known to the academia at the international level and often travels to prestigious centres of learning, he has not visited India so far. It was therefore a privilege to listen to him at the Cambridge seminar on the Contemporary British writer. The hall was packed when Steiner began to speak on "Tomorrow and Tomorrow."

In this illuminating talk, Steiner did some crystal ball gazing into the future of literature in an age of biological cloning, digital computers, and cyber narrations. Steiner's approach and allusions clearly go beyond the literary. His speech combines theoretical insights with down-to-earth documentation from the world of popular culture.

Is there a possibility of a truly planetary language, asked Steiner rhetorically. There has always been a hope in such a possibility. After all, the language Esperanto itself contained the word *espoire*, meaning "hope."

In today's context, it is perhaps the language of the Anglo-American variety that claims such a status. Nearly eighty percent of written works in Tel Aviv, Amsterdam and Munich contain translated works of Anglo-American originals. Today, said Steiner, every committed worker has to be bilingual. What will that do to the question of national literature?

Some linguists, however, predict that "the planetary Anglo-American language" itself will split up. Today, only Spanish remains a worthy competitor to English. Steiner provided some interesting statistics. According to some language analysts, for instance, Spanish is moving at a speed of 3.8 miles per year in the United States. Regional isolation does not seem possible today, in the U.S. or elsewhere in the world.

In this context, Steiner offered a series of propositions:

- Every language is a window of being . . . to the world, and poetry carries that singularity of every language.
- To think about literature tomorrow is to think about a new linguistic situation.
- We need to rethink the nature of the book because the concept of the book seems increasingly archival. Barely twelve days are given for a new novel in a bookstore. Worldwide, there seems to be a decaying situation in all serious book business.
- Over 37,000 titles come to the Library of Congress in America every year. Many of these end up in clearing houses in poorer countries.
- Traditionally, it is the bourgeoisie that owned both the ownership of publication as well as the means of reading.
- Over eighty-five percent of young Americans today cannot read without a Walkman, and few can read without what is graphically called "the flicker effect," i.e., without a television on.
- Novelists like John Updike invite readers on the web to submit alternative endings to his chapters. After all, the web, cyber space and Internet are the new ways of defining our identity.

How will the onset of the post-Gutenberg world effect our understanding of literature?

Steiner paused significantly, adjusted his lenses and trained his gaze into the future. There was little trace of doubt in his tone as he outlined the future of literary creativity:

- There will be many manifestations of orality in the future.
- Equally will there be many collective participatory modes of literary invention.

- There will be new thinking on the notion of the ephemeral. For instance, a collection of Opera Hall announcement posters was donated some time ago to the New York Public Library. These were promptly dumped carelessly in the basement. However, over 1,600 references to such sources in Joyce's *Finnegan's Wake* has today generated an unprecedented scholarly interest in such a collection.
- The crisis of literature is now to deal with the challenge posed by science. After all, very few writers like Thomas Mann are dealing with science.

  At the same time, "genetics" and again transplantation seem to radically question our notion of identity: *Who am I? What was I? What will I be?* There is also the "comic, brutal idiocy" of Viagra that touches very deeply the history of Eros. Imagine a great poem on Viagra!
- Similarly, Freud's essay on daydreaming would have agreed with Darwin's view of Shakespeare: "He is so childish!" Not a surprising conclusion, when scientists have begun to describe "consciousness as a matter of blood and sugar," and memory basically as a "neurochemical function!"
- Although immense kingdoms have opened up since Huxley's *Brave New World*, many right-thinking men show a refusal to be subjected to chemical treatment. We need help from writers in this regard. What will their contributions be?

Stephen Hawking, a follower of Newton at Cambridge, believes that we are now very close to the theory of everything. What will happen when we "hit the wall of certitude," asked Steiner.

Steiner closed his talk by narrating a poignant anecdote, a commentary on our arrogance of knowledge. Today, he said, medical science has taught us that alcoholism in parents often causes deformity in children before they are born. It is held axiomatic that mentally crippled children ought not to be born. However, we must remember the case of the German father who was an alcoholic, whose wife gave birth to two mentally crippled children successively. "Perhaps this is the curse of God," said the local priest. "Perhaps they should desist from having any more children to prevent further calamity." The father went ahead nevertheless. The result was the birth of a deaf-mute—the birth of Ludwig Von Beethoven.

"And I can never think of a world without a Beethoven," said Steiner with a flourish of his hand. Very few could have taken an audience from the horrors of the holocaust to the magic of the symphonies of Beethoven!

Steiner's diagnosis of contemporary culture at times bordered on despair, and he found insufficient literary response to the challenge posed by science in its varied manifestations. All the same, he stood for hope. We must, he concluded, constantly critique modes of thinking that militate against the literary and creative apprehensions of the world.

Education: Call for a New Definition

The crisis we face today in polity, economy and culture has its roots in education. The solution lies in educating our educators, and this, not through training camps or refresher courses, but by working on an alternate vision of education.

We all know that we are in the midst of a crisis. This crisis assails us every day on all fronts—polity, economy and culture. Few realise, however, that the cause and remedy of the crisis lies in education. Fewer still can guess that the problem involves the educators themselves.

The solution to the crisis does not lie in teacher training camps or refresher courses, State-sponsored activities linked to promotional avenues and career advancement. It is not the acquisition of more knowledge or more techniques that T.S. Eliot decried that can help us resolve the crisis in education. The solution lies in offering an alternative vision, and changing radically the mindset of the educators themselves.

Every educator is a crisis manager; of a crisis immediate or potential. What is the nature of the present crisis that the educator of tomorrow must address?

First, there is the widening gap between social mores and rapid technological exchanges. Developments in cyber space and biological cloning have profound implications, moral and ethical, that the human mind can hardly fathom. Are we doomed to be slaves of gadgetry?

Second, the collapse of our cherished ideologies—Soviet communalism, Nehruvian socialism, and even the welfare capitalism of the West. What system of polity and economy shall we adopt?

Next, there is the seeming triumph of a "globalised" economy and multinational capitalism. Cultural modes associated with these forces often come to us as threatening icons. Are we doomed to a diet of Pepsi Cola, Madonna, and Michael Jackson?

We also witness the frightening emergence of religious revivalism, and of various forms of extremism. Is mutual bloodshed and killing going to be our fate?

There is an increasing conflict between democracy as a political system seeking majority welfare versus market economy that promotes minority agenda. How shall we reconcile these conflicting interests without an authoritarian or a laissez-faire State?

The solutions to the crisis are hard to find. However, certain options can be safely ruled out. The educator of the future knows that we cannot give up science and technology for a prescientific social order. Such a longing can only be naively romantic and hopelessly unrealistic. Similarly, we cannot seek the exclusive welfare of either the majorities or minorities. These are fluid concepts and have different meanings across the vast social spectrum and cultural mosaic.

While we seek multiple identities, the ideal educator knows that exclusive identities are socially dysfunctional and positively harmful. We must pursue, therefore, several allegiances at once—the family, the community, the province, the nation, and the world.

Again, education as formal learning has strengthened the interests of the few at the expense of the many. The new approach to education must redefine the meaning of education if it has to serve the interests of the citizenry. Formal training in education requires big investments of money and manpower, which we can ill afford today.

The alternative view of education must consequently rely not on material resources but on the exciting network of relationships in society—those who impart learning in any situation—parents, elders, managers, all so-called lay persons. The rents, elders, managers, all so-called lay persons. The educators of today, as Ivan Illych has aptly suggested, have become the enemies of education. Consequently, we must save education, as the De-schooling Society argues, from the educators themselves.

How, then, do we educate the educators? The answer may be elusive, but a beginning can be made in several directions:

- We must give up the arrogant claim that the educator "knows." We must replace this claim of superiority of the educator by the humility that the student or the taught can learn on his/her own. We must involve the pupil in the actual task of learning. "The first principle of all true teaching," says Sri Aurobindo, "is that nothing can be taught." The teacher is only a guide and a pathfinder, not an instructor or a taskmaster.

- All learning must proceed, as the scientists tell us, from the near to the far, from the local to the regional, to the national, and finally to the global. The corollary to this proposition is that solutions must emerge organically from the immediate environment and must be locally tried and not imported from outside.

- The new educator combines an informality of approach with a premium on creativity. He combines firmness with flexibility, an imaginative rather than an authoritarian or bureaucratic approach. He does not decide the site of learning, but seeks the initiative of the students.

- The new educator must be an example. He must try out the solution himself before demanding it from the taught. He must always have a moral and intellectual edge. He must remember that the best authority is always the moral or spiritual authority. The best educator is one from whom the whole of life is a continuous field of learning.

- Finally, the new educator is not judgmental about men and matters. He does not place faith in the binary doctrine of exclusive choices, the morality of good and evil. He does not idealise preferred modes of feeling while demonising its opponents. Rather, he approaches all rival positions in a spirit of sympathy and understanding, with sensitivity rather than impassioned denunciation or condemnation. He believes in what Patrick J. Hill calls "a conversation of respect among men."

Critics of the new education will dismiss this new approach as soft and naïve. For it does not prepare offsprings as clones in the corporate rat race. But already, there are enough contradictions in the so-called arenas of success, both in business and in society. These must give us hope for the new system. And finally, the alternative system is not one more feather in the "progressive" cap, but perhaps the only possible way we can prevent the tragedy of the future.

University as an Apex of Intellectual, Creative Life

How shall we redefine the role of the University or higher education in India as we enter the new millennium?

The decision to de-link higher education from State subsidy has sent shock waves across the universities. Already, the Central Universities that depend almost exclusively on the UGC are in a serious financial crisis. The argument that State support of a top-heavy, elitist system has led, over the years, to a parasitical situation at the expense of badly starved primary and secondary education has, of course, strong merit. The call to make the university system self-supportive and more accountable to the community is an equally unexceptionable demand. However, several aspects of the issue call for careful consideration.

Privatisation is no magic wand or panacea to resolve the crisis that the Indian university system faces. Mere privatisation of the institutions of higher learning that does not take into account the structural factors will only make education more elitist. Worse still, it has serious implications on the fate of the humanities and the liberal arts.

The notion of the university system as a haloed centre of learning in moulding the character of individuals, in shaping the lives and destinies of people and nations, has given way today to a functional view that sees the university basically as an academic marketplace where knowledge as a commodity is bartered or sold. Logically, therefore, it is the marketplace that is the single important influence on the university today.

Intrinsic Merits

Similarly, organised systems of learning and branches of knowledge such as literature and philosophy, geography and geology, are judged not in terms of their own intrinsic merits but by the bearing such faculties may have on the power relationships that obtain in society and polity.

Such domains as the economy and the polity are constantly subject to strain and pressures. By their very nature, they respond readily to exigencies. It is natural, therefore, that institutions thriving on their sponsorship cannot boast the stability necessary for generating an alternative critique of man and society.

In recent times, the university system in the country has shown itself pathetically incapable of meeting even these limited goals of the marketplace. The cry for more science, more technology in the universities, through a surfeit of funding agencies, has not led to a commensurate economic or developmental benefit. Similarly, the creation of an ambitious CSIR, with its own chain of laboratories, paralleling the existing number of labs in the university departments, seems to indict the university system for carrying out research largely perceived as theoretical, derivative and academic.

The climate of cynicism in the university is easily explained. The academic system, as all organisations, create their own particular power structure. A quick understanding of such a structure could be more rewarding to an individual teacher than a questioning of its rationale. The scramble for more books, more papers and more seminars actually conceals a poverty of thought and genuine introspection even in the best of universities. Not surprisingly, therefore, conformism and careerism rather than independent thinking seem to be the key notes.

The crisis that the university system faces has reached a terminal stage because the system has earned for itself an irrelevance for both the public and the private sectors. The teachers as a group are not seen to make a vital contribution. Their work, seen largely as pedantic exercises, is increasingly more esoteric.

The organised State itself, not known for promoting creative and independent thinking, is only too eager to withhold support.

If higher education has to have any meaning—in howsoever a restrictive sense—it is important to ask larger questions such as the basic objectives a community places before itself, the role of the university as an apex of intellectual, creative life in realising such goals, the role that different branches of learning can and ought to play, and finally, the right kind of organisational structures that a university ought to have commensurate with its goals.

Universalisation of literacy, eradication of poverty, promotion of a humane and scientific temper and an egalitarian society, freedom of thought, expression and worship—these could be described as some of the basic goals of the society. Again, it is not as though such goals are unknown to the educational planners. But they are seldom put into effective practice.

Specialisation

The history of university education in the world reveals that a change took place in the late nineteenth century from old style college for prospective clergymen to new German type of university research and discovery of knowledge, organised into fields of specialisation and administered within specialised departments. The older English and American colleges such as Oxford, Cambridge, Harvard, Yale and Princeton laid more emphasis on character building and undergraduate education, whereas many new ones such as Johns Hopkins, Cornell and Chicago preferred the graduate and professional over undergraduate education.

Over a period, such distinctions have hardened in the university context between disciplines that are perceived as lucrative and those that are "soft," between the "pure" subjects and the applied ones. This had led to an academic caste system and a pecking order that prefers, say, computer sciences and engineering over the sciences, the sciences over the liberal arts, economics over language, literature, and so on.

Many of the disciplines such as philosophy, literature and the "pure" sciences do not have an immediate application. While it may be possible to find an immediate use for language study and economics, removing state support without providing an alternate source of funding for many of these disciplines would lead to a further decline in these vital areas.

Humanities and the liberal arts are supposed to answer basic questions that have a long term bearing upon the future of a given society. By delving deep into the issues, they are expected to provide a sense of direction to a nation or community. The answer to the problem of higher education is, therefore, not to privatise all sources of funding but to restructure the university system, especially its system of pedagogy.

A quick look at the existing system of curricula, syllabi and teaching methods followed in the present university system suggests that certain changes are long overdue. For instance, subjects could be taught as problem-oriented rather than offered as a mechanical presentation of facts, lacking a sense of context and perspective.

History could be taught not merely as a narration of religious and ethnic conflicts but also by underlining the drive towards harmony and unity in all spheres—political, economic and spiritual—latent in the Indian experiment. Philosophy might show, for instance, how to recapture the potential of native traditions for a society facing an increasing breakdown in communication. The possibilities are endless.

Such a focus would also call for the abolition of the disciplinary isolation of the present in favour of a truly interdisciplinary approach and integrated courses of study. What has so far happened in the name of such goals has been mostly a series of platitudes.

A truly multidisciplinary approach presupposes what Patrick J. Hill calls "a conversation of respect," a healthy respect for all disciplines, and a willingness to learn insights from the tradition of all areas of study. In a sense, this is not really a matter of choice. The enormous complexity of the present world, the explosion of knowledge, the increasing breaking down of the frontiers of traditional disciplines among many advanced thinkers, the problems of poverty, hunger, armament, and the threat of global holocaust—these make it compelling to have a common pool of wisdom and to be able to communicate across different barriers.

Originality

One of the concrete ways of recognising the merits of the interdisciplinary system at the university would be to reward a scholar, possibly for the best MPhil and doctoral dissertation that displays a high degree of originality and employs techniques and tools from other disciplines. Already, such an idea is in practice in many institutions such as the American Studies Research Centre (ASRC), Hyderabad, while deciding their best thesis award every year.

Even small things can help. For all the busy academic schedule, the holding of a fortnightly or monthly extension lecture where teachers, students and visitors from other disciplines/schools are invited to speak and share their ideas, is not hard to realise.

Savage Pilgrimage: Relevance of D.H. Lawrence Today

With the passage of time, D.H. Lawrence's critical and literary standing and the public response to his works have swung between extremes. In the early days, there was, on the one hand, a small nucleus of the devout followers, and on the other, a large group of titillated, broadly unsympathetic, and at times hostile, readers. Yet, he continues to be relevant even today.

It has been many decades since the British novelist D.H. Lawrence disappeared from the literary and cultural scene of Europe. But in death, far more tellingly than in life, Lawrence continues to remain a potent force in shaping the consciousness of the twentieth century.

With the passage of time, Lawrence's critical and literary standing and the public response to his works have swung between the two extremes of exaltation and denunciation. In the early days, there was, on the one hand, a small nucleus of the devout followers, and on the other, a large group of titillated, broadly unsympathetic and at times hostile readers.

But regardless of the change in taste, Lawrence continues to be relevant even today. His confirmed iconoclasm, his deeply felt critique of "received wisdom," his advocacy of a return to the primal roots of life, his plea for a restoration of our communion with Nature—all foreshadow in an uncanny manner our own anxieties in the later half of the twentieth century. Lawrence shared a holistic perspective of the human situation. He regarded the future of man as hopelessly bleak unless he learned to match his present wisdom with a radically altered perception of the world. Lawrence's life was a religious quest in the profoundest sense of the term. "My novels emerge from the depths of my religious consciousness," he once said, talking especially of his celebrated *Rainbow*. His journey did not begin with a set of preordained assumptions. It was exploratory and was therefore a challenge as well as an adventure. Like all such adventures, his quest was fraught with grave hazards and perils, "the dark night of the soul." As in most such wayfaring, his "savage pilgrimage" caused him no end of agony, but it must have been an enormous source of reward as well; the heroism that lies in the individual's act of isolation.

An extraordinary personality who contained in him the poet, the novelist, the playwright, the essayist, the travel book writer, and the amateur psychologist, Lawrence's protean self has meant many things to many readers. He has been claimed both by the Right (see Bertrand Russell, John Harrison), as well as by the Left (Raymond Williams). Clearly, Lawrence's appeal was more than literary; his deep concern for man and the future of human civilisation makes him one of the foremost thinkers of our time. To be with Lawrence, remarked Aldous Huxley, involved a voyage of self-discovery. Lawrence's affinity towards India and the Orient was strong. Though he did not actually set foot in India (he passed through Sri Lanka on his way to Australia and the New World), his philosophy seems to intersect with significant aspects of Indian thought. Lawrence's early attitude towards Hinduism was marked by prejudice, but as he grew in life and journeyed to more ancient lands such as New Mexico, his conception of religion underwent a radical change.

His early indictment of aspects of Hinduism and Buddhism for their life-denying monasticism that comes through his remarks to the Brewsters in Sri Lanka, gave way in the later years to a more considered and balanced opinion of the spiritual experience and its centrality to life. The sense of the unknown and the elemental that Lawrence experienced among the Hopi Indians of Arizona (see his *Mornings in Mexico*) and the Pueblo of Taos led him to a deeper understanding of the wisdom of many ancient traditions. As Chaman Nahal has aptly shown in his *D.H. Lawrence: An Eastern View*, Lawrence's views on the self and self-transcendence are remarkably close to the conception of the self in the Vedas. Many foreign scholars like Gerald Doherty have explored the Indian connection of Lawrence in such essays as "Connie and the Chakras" and "D.H. Lawrence's Quarrel with Buddhism." Indeed, in his letters, Sri Aurobindo remarks: "Lawrence was a yogi who had missed his way and came to a European body to work out his difficulties."

Lawrence's tirade against organised systems of thought and "censor morons" must also make a great appeal to a society like ours still seeped in many forms of repression. These include many areas of Indian life and behaviour like the penchant for an other-worldly asceticism manifest in certain strands of Indian spirituality, the avowed denial of the body while simultaneously pursuing a hedonistic culture, and above all, the espousal of poverty as a national ideal. A society that is rebelling against the stranglehold of the past must naturally turn to a prophet like Lawrence who signifies an alternative vision of man and a worldview that sees not division nor exclusion but a wholesome balance, governing human existence.

Within a brief span of 45 years, Lawrence wrote prodigiously—novels like *White Peacock*, *The Rainbow*, *Women in Love*; stories and novellas like *England my England*, *The Woman Who Rode Away* and *The Man Who Died*; travel books like *Sea and Sardinia*, *Etruscan Places* and *Twilight in Italy*; books of amateur psychology such as *Psychoanalysis and the Unconscious* and *Fantasia of the Unconscious*; many collections of poetry such as *Birds, Beasts and Flowers*, *Look We Have Come Through*; and plenty of essays that appear in the two Phoenix volumes. He was also a painter of some standing.

During his lifetime, D.H. Lawrence was disgraced because he loved and married an already married woman, Frieda Weekly. During the xenophobia of the First World War, he was persecuted and hounded out of Cornwall by his once zealous compatriots since he had a German wife, and also because he opposed the war. There was nothing to choose between a British brand of militarism and a German brand of militarism, he said. His novels like *The Rainbow* and later, *Lady Chatterley's Lover*, were publicly banned and set on fire. The continued hostility, both literary as well as personal, forced him to leave England, first for Australia and later for the New World.

Of all the literary forms, he argued, the novel is preeminently suited to depict relationships. It is the relationship between men and women, above all, that the novelist must explore. In his celebrated *Surgery for the Novel or a Bomb*, Lawrence decried the separation between philosophy and literature. Reacting strongly against the "stream of consciousness" novels of Virginia Woolf and Dorothy Richardson, Lawrence advocated a novelist like Thomas Hardy. In his essay on Thomas Hardy, Lawrence expresses his indebtedness to the Victorian master. Indeed, *Sons and Lovers*, in depicting the triangular relationship of Paul-Clara and Miriam bears a strong parallel with Hardy's Jude, Arabella and Sue Bridehead in Hardy's later novel *Jude the Obscure*.

Lawrence's views regarding the sexes are valuable. There are stages in his life and writing career when he was attracted to a dominating male ideal, but contrary to popular impression, he was not a misogynist. His men and women were not ahistorical universals, they were concretely rooted to the socio-cultural matrix. The battle of the sexes particularly attracted Lawrence. Behind such a battle, he perceived not any fundamental antipathy between men and women, but historical force at work. Thus, despite Sandra Gilbert and Elaine Showalter, or their predecessors like Kate Millett and Simone de Beauvoir, Lawrence believed in the dethronement of a domineering patriarchy. This is a constant refrain in *Lady Chatterley's Lover* as well as his later essay "We Need One Another."

Towards the end, Lawrence's interest in religion took him closer to a mystical experience. His works of the period, such as *Apocalypse*, as well as fiction and poetry are marked by deep mystical undertones. Nothing is more remarkable than the later poem *The Sleep of Death.* Its lyrical flow and haunting words resound forever in our memory:

> Have you built your ship of death, oh, have you?
> Oh build your ship of death for you will need it.
> Now in the twilight set by the invisible sea
> Of peace and build your little ship
> Of death, that will carry the soul on its
> last journey, on and on, so still
> so beautiful, over the last of seas . . .

Master of Campus Fiction: David Lodge

Campus fiction, dealing with the flaws and weaknesses of the academia, especially the professorate, has emerged as a major area of creative writing and critical study in recent years. British novelist David Lodge speaks about his campus novels, the relationship between ideology and literature, and related issues.

A relatively small but influential body of "middle brow" writing to emerge in the post-war Anglo-American world of writing is "campus fiction." Traditionally seen as cameos of campus life, these works, spearheaded by pioneers such as Kingsley Amis, Malcolm Bradbury and David Lodge, have, in recent years, moved from hotel foyers and airport lounges into the portals of the academia. Of the group that has excelled, perhaps David Lodge is best known in India.

David Lodge was educated at University College, London, and from 1976 to 1987 was Professor of Modern Literature at University of Birmingham. His novels include *The Picturegoers* (1960), *Ginger, You are Barmy* (1962), *The British Museum is Falling Down* (1965), *Changing Places* (1975), *How Far Can You Go* which won the Whitbread Book of the Year Prize in 1980, *Small World* (1984), *Nice Work* (1988), (Sunday Express Fiction Prize) *Paradise News* (1991), and *Therapy* (1995). His play *Home Truths* was presented in 1998. Lodge's critical works include *The Modes of Modern Writing* (1977), *The Language of Fiction* (1996), *Working with Structuralism* (1982), and *The Art of Fiction* (1992). He is also a former Chairman of the Booker Prize Committee.

Lodge started out by writing reports on the football matches that he went to. "Most writers," he says, "begin when they encounter literature which they want to emulate. If you enjoy reading, then you are naturally motivated to think 'well I'd like to do that myself'!" He started writing stories when he was sixteen, mostly stories of imitation, but did not publish them.

In the post-war period, many writers took job in higher education because that was an expanding field. New universities were being built and existing ones expanded. Working first for the British Council, Lodge later joined the Birmingham University and spent the next twenty years as a University teacher. Younger writers, Lodge believes, tend to write from their own experience. "I guess the older I get, the more I research my material. I write about the University because I have been a University teacher and that was my experience largely."

Lodge's first work, *Picturegoers*, was published in 1960. Named after a magazine by the same title, *Picturegoers* basically is about the local community, a cross section of suburban life, centered around the cinema and the church. The novel was received well and was quite popular.

Not all of Lodge's novels deal with the academic world. For instance, his second work is about national service in the army. The campus novel as a distinctive genre actually started in the U.S. and can be traced to Lionel Trilling and others. "The seminal British campus novel was *Lucky Jim*. There is a combination of subtle social observation of manners in the academic community, the petty rivalry, pretension and absurdity which go back to the English comical novels of Dickens and Fielding." Kingsley Amis was thus a model for Lodge, Malcolm Bradbury and many others.

Significantly, Lodge and Bradbury have often been compared. Both were colleagues at Birmingham, joining the University in the early sixties. Bradbury was a natural comic writer and wrote comic sketches in *Punch*. "Although my early writing had humour in it," Lodge said,

> It was not basically comical. It was Malcolm who encouraged me to write comedy. I have acknowledged him in *The British Museum is Falling Down*. After a while, however, it became somewhat odd for two novelists to exist in the same place, drawing upon similar material. Although remaining friends, we felt that we had to put up a geographical separation between us. It's funny that people often confuse us. People think that I have written his books and that he has written mine. Recently, for instance, I saw his first novel *Eating People is Wrong* advertised as my first novel (laughs). This is because we were both professors, both wrote books about the English going to America, and both were of the same age. We are different writers actually.

About the theme of Roman Catholicism in many of his works, especially *The British Museum is Falling Down*, he says,

> Well I was brought up as a Catholic. My mother was a Catholic. I had a Catholic education. During adolescence either you rebel against your background or you continue with it. I have remained a Catholic. I find it a definite source of ideas and material for fiction. You will find my novels a kind of skepticism about religion. In a way I find it hard to recognise *Picturegoers* now as my own. It affirms the possibility of faith in the supernatural. My last novel, *Paradise News*, on the other hand, is all about a priest who has lost his faith, although I believe religion still matters and that man cannot live by bread alone.

About similarities between Lodge and Graham Greene, Lodge acknowledged the influence of Greene that he imbibed in a book called *How Far Can You Go*. "I used Graham Greene's fiction," he says, "as a kind of index, how attitudes and thoughts for the Catholic change from one of belief and obedience to one of doubt and confusion. From 1950 till his death, Graham Greene moved from being an orthodox Catholic to an agnostic. That is how I would describe myself now."

Lodge has often portrayed characters in a hilarious manner, particularly with reference to some of the Catholic obsessions such as birth control and contraception. "When I married a Catholic," he says about his early personal life, "I was conscious about following the rules of the Church. I was struggling with the stipulation of early married life which now seems to be totally absurd. We discussed this after a certain number of years as in the case of most sensible couples."

Does he think professors and students are constantly making fools of themselves or is there an underlying comical message?

> I think all fiction is concerned in exposing flaws and weaknesses in the system of thought that pretend to be wise and powerful. The novel is essentially a subversive form. I admire the Russian theorist Bakhtin who saw the novel essentially as a carnivalesque form, as a weapon against authoritarian, totalitarian regimes. To that extent, the academia is no different from any other world in the belief that it is the most important institution in the world. Universities as institutions are supposedly dedicated to the pursuit of Truth. They value Beauty and Art. While they are dedicated to the highest human ideals, they are also staffed by human beings, who have weaknesses. Therefore, if a University professor displays lust or greed or will to power, it is morally no more faulty, absurd or funny than it would be if a politician did the same thing.

Lodge's *Nice Work* was an interesting take-off on the industrial novel of Elizabeth Gaskell and others. As he explains it, originally he wanted to write about a businessman who lived only for work and suddenly was thrown out of it. He had leisure but did not know what to do with it. Then he met a young woman from an intellectual-artistic background. As Lodge researched, he began to develop the theme involving the industrial boss and the young lecturer; the latter was an academic expert of the industrial novel of the nineteenth century, but had never been to a factory all her life. That was guaranteed to generate a certain kind of interesting frisson, just as he, the industrial boss, would be overcome by romantic infatuation. As a narrative unfolds, both become more human and vulnerable, therefore more interesting. "I think," Lodge adds, "Robin in many ways is an admirable character. She is much more human and sympathetic than her theoretical beliefs!"

Nice Work sold about 30,000 in hard cover, and in paperback around 2,00,000 or 3,00,000 copies. However, Lodge never thought of himself as a bestseller. It really started with *Small World*. "Once you sell three or four books at that level," he says, "you acquire a readership who go on buying your book. You are not interested in getting good reviews necessarily."

Much of the salesmanship, in any case, is achieved, Lodge suggests, through media hype and the building of a celebrity status. Later, this status itself is also undermined for the sake of further royalty. "I am very interested in the whole subject and this Faustian compact between the media and the literary world," he says. The typical example is the interview, which is a kind of contest. The interviewer wants to find what no one has found, and the interviewee wishes to promote his own image. Very often, there are different sexes. Newspapers would send a man to interview a woman, a woman to interview a man. Very often, it is a confession. The very situation makes the interviewee reveal and say things that he/she never intended to say. There is an element of transgression about it. It is private and yet it is not private. Where do you draw the line? Can you control it? There are traps and dangers for both parties, particularly for the interviewee, Lodge says.

How does Lodge's theoretical interests intersect with his role as a writer? "I believe," he says, "there is a semiotic relationship between the two. I often draw my ideas from academic criticism and I use them in my fiction often in comic or satirical ways. Clearly there is some influence." One could not agree more.

A Literature of Their Own: Early Literary Women of Orissa

In their search for meaning in life and literature, Oriya literary women have helped build an alternative tradition of aesthetics. The narratives of such women have an interface with the history of many progressive movements in Orissa.

In the first ever short story published in the Oriya language in 1898 by Fakir Mohan Senapati, generally acknowledged to be the father of modern Oriya fiction, Rebati, the female protagonist, displays a forbidden desire for learning and thereby seems to invite misfortune upon herself and her community in Fakir Mohan's hands. Rebati thus becomes an icon, her story an allegory for female education and emancipation. The narrative marks the beginning of a new tradition and inaugurates a new breed of women who learned to write and created a literature of their own in Orissa—Kokila Devi, Kuntala Kumari Sabat, Sita Devi Khadanga, Sarala Devi, Basanta Kumari Patnaik, Bidyut Prabha. In recording their moments of joy, sorrow, doubts and dilemmas in their poetry, prose, fiction and drama, they replicate Rebati's agonising search for education. In effect, they become Rebati's sisters.

While the experience of early literary women of Bengal like Rasundari Devi, Sarat Kumari Choudhurani, Binodini Dasi and Ashapurna Devi is fairly well known, unfortunately the same cannot be said of "the literary domestics" of Orissa whom I call "Rebati's sisters," during the late nineteenth and early part of the twentieth centuries. By "literary domestics" I mean those women who found themselves in a domestic setting and yet had literary aspirations. As Mary Kelley aptly explains: "Both in their published prose and their previously neglected letters, diaries and journals, these women reported on their own phenomenon and became unwilling witnesses to both their public events and their own private experiences."

Early women writers in Orissa date back to the medieval period and include such figures as Brindavati Dasi (who lived during the time of Sri Chaitanya), Tribhuvan Mahadevi and Nih Sanka Devi. These women and most of their followers wrote religious and spiritual poetry that eschewed the overtly political, including issues of women's concerns. For instance, Sulakshana Devi of Tigiria (born in 1829) composed a collection of poems called *Parijatamala*. Similarly, Suchitra Devi of Puri district (born in 1881) published in 1901 an anthology called *Kathalahari*, just as Annapurna Devi of Chikiti, Ganjam district (born in 1883) composed devotional songs.

While such writings by women continue to exist till today, it is only during the early decades of the twentieth century that several factors such as the movement for the preservation of the Oriya language, the rise of the Oriya regional consciousness, the advent of the Brahmo Samaj in Orissa, the campaign for widow remarriage, the legal abolition of untouchability, and the struggle for national independence, foregrounded literary women of Orissa into a hitherto closed public domain. The narratives of such women have an interface with the history of many progressive movements in the State such as the rise of female education, trade union movements, and women's participation in other forms of civic and political life.

Nineteen years after the British came to India, the first missionary schools were set up in Cuttack in 1822. This was despite the fact that the British, according to the East Indian Company Act of 1813, Section 43, had officially taken up education as part of their responsibility within the next one and a half years after 1822. The missionaries took up the management of fifteen native schools in Orissa including the English Charity School set up in 1823 in Cuttack; the East India Company took it over in 1841.

While public education in Orissa was pathetically dismal, education for women was more or less absent. Whatever education was traditionally given to them was private and confined to the home. Even this was restricted, as the editor of *Utkal Deepika* astutely observed, to the female members of the royalty and the upper classes/castes. For all others, formal education for girls was confined to a few members of the Christian community. For the first time in 1871, a school for Hindu girls was set up at Cuttack in the house of Abinash Chandra Chattopadhyaya, a school with just 13-14 students. Even in 1881, the school had registered practically no growth, nor could it catch the public imagination. The number of girls increased merely to twenty-five. This and the astonishing fact that even after the school had run for ten years at Cuttack city, only four Hindu girls were enrolled, were much regretted by the editor of *Utkal Deepika* who drew the attention of parents and urged them to send their girls to school in large numbers.

One of the first among the "literary domestics" in Orissa was Reba Ray (1876-1957). Married to the well-known littérateur and Brahmo, Sadhu Charan Ray (born 1871), Reba is credited with the founding of the Model Girls School, which later became the historic Ravenshaw Girls School, Cuttack, the cradle for the education of some of the leading literary women of Orissa. In 1903, she published a collection of poems called *Anjali*, and in 1904 an anthology of short stories called *Shakuntala*. She also founded and edited a literary journal, *Prabhat*, as well as a magazine for women.

Reba's contributions in the form of poems and stories are frequently seen in *Utkal Sahitya*, the most prominent of contemporary literary journals, edited by Biswanath Kar. Many of their poems are deeply spiritual in nature. While gender identity is hinted at here, the poems seem to carry deeply philosophical and existential undertones. "The Sound of Silence" provides a characteristic example:

In silence came I to this world

And my life will sing unceasingly.
In silence will my life forever
Her songs of silence sing
....
In silence comes the year now
And in silence now is past.
The little streams in silence
Rush along the ocean vast
In silence bloom the little buds
And in silence fade away
Their aching heart of pain
They bear in silence grey
....
Silent, shorn of strength is woman
Beside a man for ever strong
When she can't even cry for you
For fear of loud-voiced man so long
In silence then within my heart
This cry of silence will resound
O hark! My Lord and hark you well!
She at your feet in silence bound

(Translated from the Oriya *Niraba* by Maurice Shukla)

While little is known of Reba Roy's writings today, equally negligible has been the public attention paid to another literary domestic, Kokila Devi, sister of the illustrious author Laxmikanta Mahapatra of Bhadrak. Kokila (literally meaning "cuckoo," apparently so named because of her dark complexion) was widowed at an early age. She and her sister Jahnavi led an active part in the freedom struggle, social reform, and women's movement. Abjuring aristocratic comforts, Kokila felt inspired by the teachings of Gandhiji and chose to live in the Ashram that she set up amidst the so-called untouchables of the village. For Kokila, social activism went hand in hand with literary creativity. Not surprisingly, many of her works record personal dilemmas and ideological aspirations. For instance, the little known but important tale "Bilasini" centres on the so-called illicit love of a widow. The narrator's attitude to the plight of Bilasini oscillates between the two poles of empathy and disfavour. The initial meeting between Bilasini and her paramour, Jagabandhu, clearly elicits from the narrator a note of disdain: "I wonder how there could be so much of evil in such a beautiful earth laden with fruits, flowers and creepers. How could the same earth bear bestiality where the child partook nectar in the lap of the mother?" Later, however, her forsaken state evokes a different feeling from the narrator: "My heart was filled with great remorse. The sorrow was not just on account of Bilasini. It was for the helplessness of womankind in general."

Not surprisingly, Bilasini's problem is resolved at Brindavan—through a sublimation of the erotic into spiritual love, a resolution characteristic of many contemporary narratives. She becomes an object of reverence for the narrator: "My heart automatically bowed at her feet. I was stunned by what I saw. The beating of my heart stopped. After much effort, I called out at once: 'Bilasini!' Tears rolled down my cheek. My voice was choked. I looked around and spotted no one. Was I awake or asleep . . .?" (translation mine)

Kokila's achievement in *Bilasini* lies not so much in her deft handling of the ideological and emotive issue of widow remarriage, though that clearly is, in terms of her bold, frontal attack against this particular social evil. Her real skill is, however, manifest in the effortless ease with which she is able to weave in multiple styles and voices, the most important of which is the dialectic between the romantic and the social-realistic worldviews. The very opening paragraph, with its charmingly idyllic and evocative aspect of Nature, is carefully offered as a sharp contrast to the reality of Bilasini's world of isolation and despair:

> The day was nearly over. The setting sun cast an unusual glow of vermilion. Hundreds of red gold lotuses bloomed on the vast empyrean. Notes of farewell resonated in the four corners. Birds returned to their nests, their parting

melodies resounding in all directions. The indigo of the distant mountains gently merged into the vast azure. Soon, the blue of the forests turned dove grey. Hundred upon hundreds of birds hanging from the branches in clusters made the hollows of the trees look fearful. There was darkness everywhere. Darkness covered the heart. A dark curtain suddenly dropped. All became still and immobile. (translation mine)

Kokila was followed by a worthy successor, Sarala Devi. A woman who gave up her upper caste aristocratic lifestyle and plunged headlong into the women's movement and the freedom struggle, Sarala was exceptionally gifted and had a versatile personality. She was the first Oriya woman to take part in Gandhi's Satyagraha movement and was jailed at Ganjam and at Vellore in Tamil Nadu along with Durgabai Deshmukh. She joined hands with Sailabala Das, Kuntala Kumari, Reba Ray and Rama Devi. Travelling extensively within the State, she took a leading role in "The Swaraj Fund" and spearheaded the formation of a woman's association called "Mahila Bandhi Samiti."

Virtually self-taught, Sarala mastered Oriya, Bengali and English. The bulk of her writings was characterised by a deep concern over the plight of the woman in a feudal/patriarchal society. Like the other "literary domestics," Sarala too saw no contradiction between a worthy home/family life and a participation in the wider socio-political space. Even from jail, she evinces keen interest in the welfare of her "little Tikun" and chides her husband for neglecting their child. Overjoyed at the success of the women's association of Orissa, Sarala declared:

I feel gratified that my cherished dream of the past has been finally realised. It was truly beyond my expectation that the women of Utkal would one day find recognition. This is a new chapter in the history of Orissa. Which lover of the nation would not be filled with joy at seeing the raising of the woman's voice?

Sarala's literary output was truly remarkable; she had to devote time to cater to her multifaceted interests. She tried her hand in many genres including poetry, drama and fiction. However, it is mostly as an essayist and a letter writer that she excelled and put to effective use her fiery spirit as a rebel, social activist and reformer. Some of her articles were published in Bengali journals like *Debjani*. Among her published works in Oriya are *Bishwa Biplabini* (*The Great Revolutionaries of the World*) (1930), *Utkalara Nari Samasya* (*The Problems of the Women of Orissa*) (1934), *Narira Dabi* (*The Rights of Women*) (1934), *Bharatiya Mahila Prasanga* (*About the Women of India*) (1935), *Rabindra Puja* (*A Homage to Rabindranath*), and *Beera Ramani* (*The Women of Valour*) (1949).

As a close associate of Ananda Shankar Ray, who wrote both in Oriya and Bengali, Sarala was a leading member of Oriya Romanticism. She was one of the six who jointly wrote the novel *Basanti*. In *The Rights of Women*, Sarala outlines a manifesto for women's empowerment. Comparable to Mary Wollstonecraft's *Vindications of the Rights of Women*, what impresses us here is her extraordinary reading into contemporary history, law and social life in India and abroad. In voicing her indignation against the subordination of women and against marital rape. Sarala emerges as a revolutionary woman far ahead of her times. Here is Sarala quoting Justice Meccard on matters like marital rape and the right of woman over her own body and reproductive self:

> I maintain that the woman's body can never be owned by her husband. It's her own property and not her husband's. She can leave her husband at her will; she can select her business or join the political party of her choice. She has full rights to decide whether or not she is going to have a child and at what point in time. No one can keep a woman under control on the basis of the fact that he is married to her. The woman of this country has won independence; she

is a citizen and not a slave. One does not get the pleasure of married life from the codes of rules and regulations. The success of marriage depends on mutual compassion, mutual consideration, mutual forgiveness, mutual sacrifice, and above all, a mutually shared morality. (translation mine)

Other literary women of Orissa followed a somewhat different trajectory depending on the circumstances of their life and the vocations they followed. For instance, many Oriya Brahmo women like Narmada and Pratibha Kar, illustrious daughters of Biswanath Kar, the editor of *Utkal Sahitya*, wrote translations and adaptations of texts from Western literature such as those by Leo Tolstoy. Narmada's pieces, such as "Dilemma," dealing with the virtue of religious tolerance and based on a story by Tolstoy, appeared in *Utkal Sahitya* in 1913. Later, many such tales were published in a collection called *Prasad* (*The Palace*).

There is much in common between Sarala Devi and another distinguished literary woman of Orissa, Kuntala Kumari Sabat, who alone can match Sarala's stature as an emancipator, activist and literary artist. Born into a Christian family, Kuntala's parents were Daniel and Monica Sabat. Kuntala's story, at once tragic and inspiring, has many noteworthy features. She spent parts of her childhood in Burma, where her father was a physician. Later in life, she practised medicine in Delhi and took an active part in the "All India Women's Conference." Thus, her writings reveal the working of a composite culture and exile sensibility. The evocation of the ancestral Hindu memory plays a significant part in many of her writings. While Kuntala betrays no anxiety regarding minority faith vis-à-vis the larger world of Hindu symbols, customs and folklore that populate her literary landscape, the question of faith and creativity in Kuntala's calls for a closer study.

Kuntala wrote extensively in prose and poetry. She is undoubtedly the best known of the literary women in Orissa, and her works like "Shefali Prati" ("For Shefali Flower") are frequently anthologised. It is poems like "Shefali Prati" and "Tara

Prati" and the publication of the poetry collection called *Unchawasa* that brought her into the literary forefront. Later, she published novels like *Kaliboohu* (*The Dark Daughter-in-Law*), *Parashmani* (*The Touch Stone*), *Natundi* (*The Woman of Many Tongues*), as well as *Raghu Arakhita*.

Kuntala combined several seemingly contradictory traits in her personality. Her deeply sensitive nature, her concern over the plight of her land Utkal as well as the freedom of India, her empathy for the dispossessed and the underdog in society, and her support for the cause of women's emancipation are seen in her poetry and prose. At times, a single text seems to contain several such interests. She seemed to combine effortlessly the concerns of her inner, spiritual life with those of the outer world of turmoil and conflict. The best of her poetry, as in the case of "Shefali Prati," is marked by a deeply lyrical flow and spontaneity and underline an attempt at self-definition.

That Kuntala played an important role at the national level is evident from contemporary accounts. Her life formed the basis of a novel in Hindi called *Kalyani* by Jainendra Kumar. Despite all this, sadly, Kuntala is little known at the national level today.

Kuntala had an untimely and tragic death. She died in childbirth and left behind a legacy that became a source of inspiration to many literary women in Orissa. There were women like Nirmala Devi and Harapriya Devi who wrote powerful poems of the inner and outer experiences. Others like Sushila Devi published in the journal *Shankha* (1947) partition stories like "They too are Humans," while others like Nandini Satpathy, née Panigrahi, in the post-independent period responded to ideological issues such as the trade union movements and the other progressive movements of the day. For instance, Nandini's "Call of the Chimney," first published in the leftist journal *Sanket*, depicts the poignant tale of Siba who is forced to give up his proud sickle in favour of a job in a distant factory. "The chimney's call," the author says, "can only lead to destitution and unmitigated disaster." Yet, the ending of the story is not entirely bereft of hope and optimism:

With the limp child on his shoulder, Siba got down and holding Phula's hand plunged into the darkness and rain. In a soft subdued voice, Phula said: "Shall we never return?"

"Yes, we shall, one day. Only after ending the line of the Masters and the Saviours!"

A blast of cold wind from the North drove them to the other pole of the world into the arms of millions of creatures like Siba! (translation mine)

Similarly, literary domestics like Sailabala Das and Bidyut Prabha Devi lent a powerful woman's voice in poetry and prose writings. Sailabala was the first woman from Orissa to travel to England for higher studies. Her accounts of the West were serialised in *Utkal Sahitya*, and her autobiography that records her political and literary life was published in 1956. Similarly, Bidyut Prabha, who wrote basically in the Romantic mould, distinguished herself by many poems that capture the predicament of the literary domestic. For instance, "Dilemma" captures vividly the conflict between the reality of domestic living versus the urge for literary creativity. The questions are sharp and offer an indictment of the hold of patriarchy:

Am I a bonded labourer?
Am I to be sold daily
Only for this house?
Work, work and more work
From morning till night
Tell me,
Is there nothing else
To life?

However, there seems to be little choice for the woman. For, as she says:

Writing is the balm
For all my pain

It's the glory of my sorrow
Writing is rain-soaked woods
It's the music of cloudbursts
During the month of Shravana!
I wish I could speak of
The joy that gathers in my heart
Like a flame
In the mouth of a storm
My poetry
A luminous lamp. (translation mine)

Thus, from Kokila to Kuntala down to Nandini and Bidyut Prabha, Oriya literary women have covered a great distance. In their relentless and agonising search for meaning in life and literature, in their defiance of patriarchal orthodoxy and received wisdom, they helped build an alternative tradition of aesthetics and politics in Orissa. Like the prototypical Rebati, they strove steadfastly after knowledge and identity, and formed a sisterhood of rare distinction.

Fulbright and International Education

The Fulbright Program in educational and cultural exchanges between India and America celebrated its golden jubilee in 1999. Many of its beneficiaries read like the "Who's Who" of India's top leadership. As this unique programme is poised to enter the new millennium, beset by "donor fatigue" and depletion of the Indo-U.S. Rupee Fund, I offer new rationales for strengthening it.

A major nationwide exercise was recently undertaken by the United States Educational Foundation in India (USEFI), the binational Fulbright Commission, on the eve of the fiftieth anniversary of this prestigious programme in educational exchange. The public debate was carried out as part of a larger effort to acquaint lawmakers in India and America with the role the programme has played in further promoting mutual understanding between the two nations. A key question is: what could be the new rationales for such exchanges in the nineties and how could we materially support them?

The Indo-American Fulbright exchanges date back to an executive agreement between Prime Minister, Nehru, and the U.S. Ambassador, Loy P. Henderson, on 2 February 1950. However, sponsored or institution-backed travels, especially in the West, go back to an earlier era and share points of convergence with the colonial enterprise. The rapid growth of area studies, the introduction of foreign language schools and centres for the study of colonial societies—innocuous and desirable in themselves—were actually prompted for the most part by the need to generate a favourable climate for conducting diplomacy, commerce, business and war. Later, more honorific manifestations of support by private enterprises for exchange activities came in the form of private foundations such as those by Cecil Rhodes in South Africa, and Henry Ford or John D. Rockefeller in America. A judicious combination of business interest and social altruism marked the approach of this era of exchanges.

Government-funded exchange activity, as it is known today, probably owes its genesis to the realisation of the role cultural diplomacy could play in shaping foreign policy in the contemporary world. The new drive for educational and cultural exchange seems to have been hastened by the world situation in the post-1945 era and the onset of the Cold War in 1949.

While the Fulbright Program owes its inception to a uniquely idealistic vision that sought the removal of cultural mistrust through the promotion of mutual understanding, it cannot be denied that much of the governmental support in the U.S. in the field of educational and cultural exchange was harnessed for what came to be known as the preservation of "the American way of life" or serving the cause of the Free World. The purposes of American educational and cultural activities abroad actually enjoy a wider mandate and are seen to serve five major goals—the lacing together of educational systems; the improvement of the context of communication; the disciplining and extending of international and intellectual discourse; international educational development; and finally, the furtherance of educational and cultural relations as ends in themselves.

I wish to suggest that a key task for new thinking on exchange activity in the post-Cold War era, especially in the American context, must be to consider whether or not the potential for federal support is exhausted by the so-called winning of the ideological war. Is it possible that the so-called "donor fatigue" in exchange activity such as the Fulbright could be on account of some factors other than the supposed loss of American interest in world affairs, and consequently, the onset of the new mood of neo-isolationism? If the American support for exchanges in the past had rallied around the cause of individual freedom, held synonymous with the American way of life, then what could be the new bases of support, the new rationale for the Fulbright exchange in the post-Cold War era? For, unless we quickly discover the new grounds, we shall forfeit our material and moral support base, our constituency of appeal.

It seems to me, therefore, that the strategy for discovering new rationales for exchange activity must underlie all the five key objectives mentioned earlier. These have not lost their ability despite the passage in time, nor their relevance today. Secondly, the upsurge of conflicts today—ethnic, religious and economic; from Rwanda, Kabul (Afghanistan) to Jakarta (Indonesia)—is the biggest threat to world peace and stability, and therefore, must seize the conscience of international educational planners in civil society. Thirdly, the rise of the unipolar world, the globalisation of economy and culture also seem to militate against the ethics of plurality, an essential prerequisite for democratic living everywhere. Progressive opinion must therefore conclude that the attempt to create a new world order by steamrolling all variations in lifestyles into an all-effacing commonality would only lead to cultural alienation and newer sources of dissonances. The spirit guiding exchange in the new millennium must instead be backed by the argument that national interest is best served when international assistance is used not as a tool of foreign or economic policy, but as the primary means of creating goodwill and understanding. These are always translated in the long run into effective economic activity.

There are other rationales for exchanges in the nineties and beyond. The sharing of resources, technologies and cultural tools can no longer be perceived as another feather in the altruistic cap that nations like to wear as image-building exercises. Instead, we might argue that such measures could actually ensure the survival of the very nations that command respect and power today. For, the basic drive in industrial capitalism remains the same, namely, how to find newer markets for goods and services, a proposition that is best realised by a balanced and equitable interaction. In other words, we must strive for newer forms of exchange compatible with the kind of world we inhabit today.

Given these rationales behind exchanges in 2000 A.D. and beyond, what could be the fresh sources of material support? To begin with, government support can still remain our best bet. The beneficiaries of the programme in America and elsewhere, through words and deeds, must demonstrate the importance of new rationales for exchange not so much as activities of moral and idealistic significance but as measures that seek the vital wellbeing and health of American society, economy and polity, as indeed of societies elsewhere. We need to reinforce the network of contacts in the government, media and citizen groups in India and the U.S.

Further, in a world of depleted public funding, we would do well to create bonds or synergy among sister foundations, many of which, such as the Ford, MacArthur or Rockefeller, seek to serve goals similar to the Fulbright. For these, more than logistics, we need to overcome the narrow mindsets and the arrogance that all bureaucracies breed among their functionaries. We must overcome the self-righteous insularity that effectively blocks cooperative action among different organisations.

The argument that a determined effort ought to be made to involve the private sector is, of course, sound. However, utmost care should be constantly taken so that the idealistic base or mission of a programme like the Fulbright exchange is never compromised by alignment or over-reliance on companies that may have regressive business or commercial interests.

A change in the executive agreement between India and the U.S. is certainly called for. However, we must ask what is responsible for the resistance to such an amendment from the host country, aside from the usual suspicion and obduracy that a weaker partner always displays towards a stronger and more powerful nation. There are many binational features that distinguish the Indo-U.S. Educational Exchange Act. These must rightly be highlighted to the Indian lawmakers and public representatives as well as the media. Similarly, there are features that also create apprehensions, especially when the sources of funding are the American Government, and are channelled through an American information agency.

Without being defensive, perhaps we need to take a fresh look to see whether we have adhered to all the provisions of the Binational Executive Act. Ultimately, there is the substitute for transparency in functioning and behaviour for popular acceptance of any such activity.

The USEFI has made impressive progress in fund raising through joint ventures, cost sharing, and partnership programmes. Yet, many sources still remain untapped. Ultimately, fund raising remains a highly professional activity. It may be advisable to create a special wing of the USEFI with a separate designated official. Help could always be sought from the Fulbright alumni—C. Rangarajan, Girish Karnad, Armaity Desai, Raja Chelliah, G. Ram Reddy and others, especially those in the corporate sector.

Finally, it must be said that educational exchange is destined to play a greater role in the coming future. We must approach the current crisis with courage and conviction. It is time the Americans realised what Senator Fulbright wrote in *The Price of Empire*:

> Of all the joint ventures in which we might engage, the most productive, in my view, is educational exchange . . . educational exchange is not merely one of these nice but marginal activities in which we engage in international affairs, but rather from the standpoint of future world peace and order, probably the most important and potentially rewarding of our foreign policy activities.

The Virtue of Aloneness

The more we condemn and the more we abuse, the more polarised we become. We have that much less space for a dialogue.

Ours is essentially a tragic age. There is of course a peculiarity to our own tragedy: unlike the older tragedies, the destruction of Pompeii, the disappearance of Atlantis, or the outbreak of the medieval plague, our tragedy is less of Job, the Biblical character, and more of Prometheus, the Greek hero. There is a lesson here that has probably not dawned on us. The post-Renaissance Cartesian enlightenment principle armed man with the confidence to make a rational choice. The choice was dramatically manifest in the great social, political and ideological experiments, democracy, capitalism, socialism, communism. However, while freedom and rationality have been emancipatory, they have paradoxically turned out to be a curse as well.

Nowhere is this tragedy, this curse, more visible than our fanatical faith in organised thinking and action. Religions, old and new, have relied on such faith, and continue their trail of bigotry and destruction. Never mind the power of revelation and the promise of the kingdom of god upon earth. Similarly, Bolshevik communism rose against the unprecedented tyranny of the Tsarist regime and spawned, equally tragically, the horror of the Stalinist era. One form of evil replacing the other.

And notice where such blind faith in rationality and science, in organised ideology and action have led us. Yesterday it was laissez-faire capitalism. Then came the death of the individual and affirmation of the truth of the collectivity, swiftly followed by the return of the individual again. An endless ritual of deification and desecration. Of course, the newer version of the old drama has its own repertoire and denouement. To miss these essential differences would be to be blind to the great outgrowth of the media and their diabolical uses by the organised groups, most of all by the political elite and the organised state. Print capitalism and the culture industry have become an explosive mix with urbanisation and industrialisation. Consequently, the vast destabilisation has proved to be a fertile ground for organised ideologies.

And all the while, the irony is lost upon us; the more zealously we plunge into action with a new slogan, a new cry, a new formula, a new shibboleth, the more we advocate one kind of authoritarianism to defeat another kind of fascism. The more we arm the power-mad state and its equally intoxicated gendarmerie in order to save us from the radical, subversive fringe of the Left and the Right, the more we slide into the abyss.

And all the while, we are held under the hypnotic spell of modern ideology. It comes in a packaged form. You have the option to choose one package from the other. In effect, making no real choice. For selectivity is out. Like a packaged TV programme beamed at passive viewers, today's ideological messiahs of a mandir or a mosque, "cultural nationalism" or "social justice," want our total loyalty or nothing. To such a mind, labelling comes easy. All labelling is a substitute for genuine introspection, essentially a mask for our inadequacy.

Progressive-reactionary, secular-communal, feminist-sexist. Not that these terms do not have their uses. Only, today's discourse makes them less descriptive and more judgmental and condemnatory.

The more we condemn and the more we abuse, the more polarised we become. We have that much less space for a dialogue and persuasive action, for our ability to lead the warring members of our own being, let alone the question of the whole community.

The answer suggested is not cynical despair or quietistic escape. But a faith in action and a commitment that emerge from a state of reflection. At least for those at the vanguard who claim to lead. So long as egalitarianism and solidarity elude us, so long will ideology play a role.

The first lesson we learn is never to give unquestioned blind allegiance to any vocal, exclusive creed, whether religious or secular. For all battle for changing the world, essentially and ultimately, begins with the self, the monster that lies deep within each one of us. Tackle this monster first, then we can look for lesser goblins and horrors. Gandhi's Hind Swaraj, his plea for self-reliance in deed and thought, has not lost its timeless relevance. There is enough in it even for lesser mortals like us.

Next, we look at each issue sympathetically and honestly—does it serve a partisan end or a collective good? The belief that the more shouting we do and the more self-righteously condemnatory we become, the closer we are to the goal is a fallacy of the highest order.

The temptation to join a cherished ideological group or a bandwagon is, of course, great. But ultimately, it leaves us vanquished, for no society has solved yet the basic economic dilemma—too few resources and too many wants. Only by deep reflection can newer tragedies be averted. Ideology was a tool, today it has become a Frankenstein monster.

Cracked Goodwill: Cultural Factors in Indo-U.S. Relationship

Indo-American goodwill, painstakingly built over the years through people-to-people contact, is being eroded by the recent spate of partisan outbursts after Pokhran II. While economic and strategic factors are at the core, it is the cultural factor that may hold an answer to the present impasse. This is not surprising if one looks at why the U.S. failed in China and Vietnam. Why is it, then, that the U.S. seems oblivious to cultural factors while passing judgement?

Official American reaction to the Indian nuclear explosion has gone far beyond the acceptable rhetoric of anger and betrayal. Policy differences among mature nations are often recognised and articulated with a sense of firmness and stridency. Much of the congressional tirade has, however, touched an all-time low in terms of contempt and distain towards India. Some like Jesse Helms, current Chairman of the Senate Foreign Relations Committee, scoff at India's claims to greatness in the face of all its pervasive "poverty and squalor." Such partisan outbursts no doubt appeal to the right-wing anti-Third World constituency in the West, increasingly vocal today even in the mainstream American media, but they deeply damage the cause of Indo-American goodwill built so painstakingly over the years through people-to-people contact. While current analysis is riveted on the political, economic and strategic factors between the two countries, it is perhaps cultural factors that hold an answer to the present impasse.

While culture is often seen universally as a soft option, cultural factors, or failure to grasp their importance, have often played a decisive role in shaping American foreign policy goals. There is ample evidence that shows that the failure of the American policies in China during the forties, and in Vietnam in the fifties, basically stemmed from cultural ignorance. As Harold Issacs aptly suggests: "Americans of all persuasions were ill-equipped to understand China in terms suited to the circumstances and traditions of their ancient culture."

To enter into a culture is to be able to hear, in Lionel Trilling's memorable phrase, "its special hum and buzz of implication." As Charles Frankel observes:

> A primary purpose of educational and cultural exchange is to become aware of other's cultural codes and of our own—to bring to the surface the context of unspoken facts and assumptions within which their words and their notions, and ours can be correctly interpreted.

Thus, when Jesse Helms heaps ridicule upon India, he probably does not realise how offensive he is being to the spirit of an older civilisation.

So heavy has been the price for Americans on account of such colossal cultural ignorance that one is genuinely puzzled at its persistence even today. It was a fatal mistake for the U.S. Administration to ignore the early messages of its envoys in China during Mao's agrarian revolution and his long march to power when he fought against the Kuomingtang. In a series of messages sent through the U.S. diplomats and newspapermen in China, Mao had sought the assistance of American private enterprise for building the infrastructure of China, an appeal that fell on deaf ears, so strong was the anti-Communist lobby in the State Department then. In "Crippled Giant," American Senator J. William Fulbright, one-time Chairman of the Senate Foreign Relations Committee, describes America's tragic slide into Vietnam relating a conversation Ho Chi Minh had with Major Frank

White, an officer in the Office of Strategic Services (OSS) in 1946. It was one of the many appeals made by Ho Chi Minh for self-determination in accordance with President Woodrow Wilson's principles, starting with the Paris Peace Conference in 1919. In Fulbright's view, nationalism in the Third World was not to be equated with anti-Americanism, a position that would cost him dear. As Athan Theoharis discloses in his *Secret Files of J. Edgar Hoover* (1991), not only was Fulbright investigated by the Federal Bureau of Investigation by a secret presidential directive from Lyndon Johnson, earlier he even lost the coveted Secretary of State post to Dean Rusk during President Kennedy's tenure.

It is not that the American establishment is unaware of the importance of cultural factors in conducting diplomacy, and the need to show sensitivity to Third World countries. Though some American administrations have argued that the services by educational institutions in foreign fields necessarily mean a drain on resources that would otherwise be available at home, most agree that the federal government should occupy an important place in such matters. As Charles Frankel declares:

> To the extent that the United States Government gave the support and encouragement under conditions that preserve the autonomy and dignity of these institutions, it announces that our society regards them not only as instruments of policy but as the independent expressions of a free civilisation to be prized as ends in themselves.

Today, the official American cultural activities encompass a formidable arena. They include the worldwide network of the United States Information Agency (USIA) created by a Congressional Act by President Eisenhower during the mid-fifties to combat the Soviets during the height of the Cold War. They also include, more significantly, a host of educational and cultural exchanges supported by the U.S. federal government, the most prestigious of which is the binational Fulbright Programme (it celebrated its fiftieth anniversary in 1996 at the international level). With an amazing 2,50,000 scholars worldwide, the programme, in the language of a Cambridge don, has effected "the largest movement of scholars across the face of the earth ever since the fall of Constantinople." In India, the programme owes its inception to an executive agreement by Prime Minister Nehru and U.S. Ambassador Loy P. Henderson in 1950. Over the years, it has produced roughly 10,000 scholars almost equally divided between the Indians and Americans.

The irony of the situation is that while the American Congress makes a commitment to cultural exchange through an annual appropriation in order to promote mutual understanding, the same Congress, during times of crisis, treats the result of educational and cultural exchange as totally redundant. More surprising is the factor that the American diplomatic service, that often draws upon academics and think tanks in the private sector, seems to be totally oblivious to cultural factors while pronouncing judgements. In India, a good number of Fulbright scholars currently occupy positions of power and eminence at the national level. Does the American administration at home or their establishment in South Asia ever bother to elicit their perception of the matter?

Meanwhile, images of India in the post-Pokhran II period in the American media continue to replicate those that Isaacs had lamented about three decades back:

> Sacred cows roaming the streets; mobs of religious fanatics hurling themselves into the Ganges; naked ascetics; scrawny fakirs on nails; the multi-armed goddess; the burning ghats; the skull-laden figures of Kali; Benares; obscene Hindu culture; phallic symbols and erotic carvings on the temples . . .
>
> A debased, hopeless sort of religion; a complicated alien mess; mystic nonsense; stupid taboos; horrible practices in a clutter of cultural dead weights; a benighted, superstitious,

> fatalistic philosophy; fanatical barbarous religiosity; the elevation of animal life above the human . . .

As Selig S. Harrison argues in his article "Dialogue of the Deaf," Americans make a sharp distinction between India and China as power factors in world affairs. The National Opinion Research Centre in the U.S., for instance, found an underlying orientation towards India that emphasised its "backwardness" and "military impotence" together with a belief that China has been "economically more successful." According to a Potomac Associates Study, China was favoured over India, despite the former's obvious suppression of democracy, by a two-to-one margin with regard to economic progress and political stability. Again, in a Gallop Poll sponsored by the Chicago Council of Foreign Relations, Americans were asked to rate other countries on the basis of vital interests. India ranked at the bottom of the list of twenty-two countries!

In reality, however, as a World Bank comparison has shown, India's overall development record is on par with that of China, and in some respects has been more favourable. Further, the image of a "militarily impotent" India is simply not true. New Delhi has the third largest standing army in the world, it is making more and more of its own military equipment, and is rapidly extending its naval reach over the Indian Ocean.

Indeed, as Harrison aptly points out, the U.S. attitude towards India has been largely shaped by a series of misconceptions. For instance, the sources of the much more heavily negative American images of India, Harold Isaacs concluded, were rooted in "the Hindu religiosity that repelled conventionally Christian Americans" and

> the effect of relative cultural value, the Chinese being seen as closer, pragmatic, down to earth, hard-headed, and the Indians or more particularly the Hindu, as much more exotic, much more violently different, as indeed the Hindu

> culture is from Anglo-Protestant and most other forms of Western culture.

Similarly, Isaacs observed that Nixon's great esteem for Yahya Khan, former General of the Pakistani army and former President,

> fits snugly into the long established pattern of contrasting ways in which Hindus and Muslims were perceived by British ruler types. It has to do with seeing the Muslims as a more upstanding, athletic, martial breed as contrasted to the prevailing image of the Hindu as weak and puny.

We see a similar assessment of the Hindus and Muslims as contrasting types in Kissinger's influential *White House Years*.

Likewise, the 1976 Asia Society Study, "Asia in American Text Books," cited widespread distortions in the treatment of Hinduism in elementary and high school texts. Hinduism, reported Kenneth Morgan, was depicted "almost entirely in terms of caste, neglecting its rich artistic and ritualistic aspects." McKim Marriot substantiated the same view of caste on a detailed critique of twenty-seven texts. According to another contribution, cows were uniformly depicted as "unproductive and parasitic animals, ignoring the fact that they generally eat chaff rather than human food, as well as their role in the economy as a source of labour in ploughing, hauling, irrigation and transport, and as a source of dung for fuel and fertiliser." (*Conflicting Images: India and the Unites States*, 1990, pp. 45-62)

Despite the American people's admiration of Gandhi's creed of non-violence, the American support for the freedom struggle in India against British imperialism, and the American admiration of the Indian democratic experiment, it has to be admitted that much of the contemporary American misperception of India has deep cultural roots. For instance, Stanley Hugh, an editor of the *Readers' Digest*, typified an influential statement in his 1978 book *A Waking World: Christianity Among the Non-White Races*:

> There would be poverty in India without Hinduism, as there is in China, but not such despair. Hinduism has written it indelibly on the consciousness of the Indian people that the lot of those who suffer is irremediable. And it has created a structure of society that is an effective guarantee of the truth of that condition . . . Hindu society has had neither the ideal nor the incarnation of a good Samaritan. . . . It is there that the real issue arises between India and the Christian West.

Clearly, such images do not promote closer understanding and do not endear the Americans to India. A prolonged standoff between India and the U.S. is in the interest of none. Despite differences in approaches to politics, economy and security, the two nations must quickly resolve their differences. It took the U.S. more than three decades to reverse its China policy. It is time they showed a greater sensitivity to India in word and deed. It is both significant and ironical that in the long diplomatic history of what Dennis Kux describes as "estranged democracies" only two U.S. ambassadors have captured the hearts of Indians—J.K. Galbraith and Chester Bowles. It is not their voices that you hear today. Fortunately, both Clinton and Kissinger do not favour India's isolation.

Perhaps Jesse Holms would do well to read the speeches of his worthy predecessor from Arkansas: "We Americans will have learnt the fundamental lessons of liberal education," Fulbright said wisely, "when we fully grasp that it is not possible to reshape the world in the American image."

The Future of American Studies

The institutional crisis, such as the one about the future of the ASRC, marks an epistemological disorder. This appears to have been precipitated by a series of developments in the fields of American demography, culture and academic theory.

What does the threatened closure of institutions like the American Studies Research Centre (ASRC) at Hyderabad really signify? Perhaps a benign indifference among the lay public; for the intellectual elite, one window less to the world; and for the global Super Power, a diminishing evidence of its once powerful cultural outreach.

The crisis is often ascribed in popular mind to the decline in United States federal support for cultural activities abroad. It seeks to mark the onset of a mood of neo-isolationism in the Congress and the revival of the older adage that the taxpayer's money is better spent at home rather than abroad. After all, it is argued, the Cold War was over, and with it has perhaps ended the need to maintain the cultural networks such as the United States Information Agency (USIA) for the spread and visibility of American culture abroad.

It seems to me, however, that the institutional crisis, such as the one over the future of the ASRC, marks a deeper epistemological disorder. This appears to have been precipitated not by conspiratorial machinations of subversive forces, characteristic of the Soviet era. Rather, a series of developments in the fields of American demography, culture and academic theory seems to have led to this crisis.

At its heart, many believe, is the notion of "American exceptionalism." Clearly, the American self-perception of the uniqueness of their national culture and its mission abroad has had profound consequences. This "exceptionalism," as defined by American theorists, has had various manifestations—"the frontier experience" of Charles Turner, "The American Adam" of R.W.B. Lewis, "homoeroticism" of Leslie Fiedler, the New England Puritan imagination of Ivor Winters, and many such single-category definitions of the American literary or cultural canon.

However, America's claim to being a supreme role model is no longer an uncontested fact. Self-determination for the individual and cultural groups is a growing maxim in international living today. More fundamentally, however, this phase marks an increasing distrust in the traditional consensus in America over what constitutes the American "national" culture. Nowhere is this more visible today than in the changing profile of American Studies as a discipline.

One of the most significant developments in recent critical approaches within the U.S. has been the uncovering of excluded zones among the cultural diversities within the U.S. Once suppressed and marginalised, these differences were subsumed in the traditional American Studies programme under the rubric of an over-arching commonality.

Nationality has traditionally been constructed on the basis of "territorial imagination." The approach to nation formation in America tended to assume that the common national culture, perceived by the elite as monolingual and Eurocentric, would assimilate the immigrant experience into the so-called Melting Pot. Instead, as John Carlos Rowe argues convincingly, "Recent approaches have stressed hybridites that have occurred historically among the many cultures constituting the U.S. Attention to these hybridities," he maintains, "requires scholars to look at the multiple cultural influences involved in important social formations; such cultural complexity is often invisible when historical changes are viewed primarily in terms of the assimilation of 'minor' cultures to a 'dominant' social system."

As a corollary, therefore, new approaches to American Studies attempt to read the U.S. in an increasingly multilingual and multicultural context. Those like Arthur Schlesinger Jr. and E.D. Hirsch who advocate the Eurocentric base of American culture are, of course, still there in the discipline. However, pioneering critics like Werner Sollors, Max Shell and others working through the Longfellow Institute at Harvard have recently published *The Longfellow Anthology* that comprises the first systematic and culturally significant works written in what is now the U.S., and published in languages other than English. Sollors effectively shows that the claim of monolingualism of the removal of illiteracy and civic cohesion in America is at best a myth. If anything, the cultural history of the American immigrants reveals that these newcomers quickly picked up the English language while retaining their original tongue. Likewise, Paul Lauter demonstrates that the foreign language requirement for graduate programmes often predictably preferred the more valorised French and German rather than the languages of the immigrant population such as Spanish, Portuguese, Chinese, Japanese, Korean and Vietnamese, not to mention the near-total neglect of the native American language.

A key task for the refashioning of American Studies is, therefore, to work out the impact of new theoretical approaches such as phenomenology, structuralism, post-structuralism, and what is loosely termed as post-colonial and cultural studies in general. The ideal way of looking at these new developments is not to treat them as antagonistic to the discipline of American Studies, but complementary to its primary task, namely the redefinition of the American culture and identity.

The role of the American State in the selective appropriation of immigrant experience has been documented in much of the recent scholarship in American Studies. For instance, in *The Politics of Culture on the Shadow of the Capital*, critic Lisa Lowe brilliantly unmasks the contradictions between the emergence of the American economy in search of cheap labour, and the role of the political State that ensured "the disenfranchisement of existing labour forces to prevent capital accumulation" by groups of Chinese, Japanese, Filipino and South Asians. It is now being acknowledged, for instance, that through a series of regressive legislations such as those relating to the Chinese in 1882, South Asians in 1917, Japanese and Koreans in 1924, and the Filipinos in 1934, the American State denied political space and civic rights to coloured immigrants, while the people of European descent were accepted in an effort to create a homogeneous White culture. Thus, it may be appropriate to conclude that "immigration has been historically a locus of racialisation and a primary site for the policing of political, cultural and economic membership in the U.S. Nation State."

It is thus apparent that American Studies, whether at home or abroad, must increasingly adopt a comparative or cross-cultural framework. It must attempt to study the multi-ethnic literatures of the U.S. It must widen its frame of reference and actively seek perspectives about America and its diverse cultures from other societies rather than exporting the so-called definitive knowledge of America produced within the U.S.

One of the corollaries of the premise is the founding of what is known today as MELUS, or The Society for the Studies of the Multi-Ethnic Literature of the United States. It was founded in 1973 "out of anger," says Katherine Newman, one of its exponents, because a valuable session on African-American Literature was presented in a part of a corridor of a New York hotel where the Annual Convention of the Modern Language Association was taking place. The MELUS India founding conference took place between 8-9 October, 1998, in Hyderabad, and has generated a great deal of scholarly interest in these multi-ethnic literatures of the U.S.

Thus, to come back to our opening, there is a sense in which the crisis in American Studies coincides with the crisis over the future of the ASRC. In both, the crisis can be turned to our advantage. The ASRC could increasingly orient itself to research of the comparative kind. The new mission of the Centre could be to "facilitate," as a recent approach paper suggests, "mutuality and exchange on issues of common concern between India and the U.S." For this, the ASRC could not only sustain the best collection of U.S. materials in Asia, but also broaden the collection in certain thrust areas to include Indian and international materials in order to provide a full and comparative perspective on these topics. The change will surely lend it a greater rootedness to our own soil and invite funding support from Indian agencies.

The future of American Studies revolves around the question of identity politics and the rhetoric of diversity. These remain as some of the crucial challenges before nationalism and post-nationalism today. It is only by refashioning the discipline of American Studies and providing appropriate institutional support systems such as the ASRC in India, that we can hope to arrive at some of the answers to the vexing questions of contemporary society and culture.

Who's Afraid of Shakespeare?: The Bard in the Classroom

A debate in Britain, the home of the Bard, raises the question of the suitability of the Master for school children.

Something, it seems, is amiss with the bard of Stratford. The young, white headmistress of a neighbourhood school in London that caters to the deprived sections, recently stopped children in her care from witnessing a public staging of *Romeo and Juliet*. The play, argued the teacher, glorifies "heterosexual love" and "male machismo," and what can be more "politically correct" than to save the young minds from such pernicious influences!

But Shakespeare is different! He is a haloed institution containing timeless truths of man and society. He has, after all, long been the proof of the supremacy of British culture and its self-appointed civilising mission in the colonies.

Does Shakespeare promote sexism, heterosexual love and male machismo in *Romeo and Juliet* and elsewhere? Is *The Tempest* an apology for racism and colonialism? Other venerated classics like Conrad's *Heart of Darkness* have been attacked in recent times, for instance, by Chinua Achebe. Why should Shakespeare, one might argue, be spared? Furthermore, should "objectionable" plays be staged with state funding? Similarly, the "dark lady" of the bard's Sonnets points to male bonding and homoeroticism. Is there a renewed case for banning Shakespeare by the resurgent homophobia?

What is the real fight about? The real fight is not about Shakespeare; it is about the inclusion and exclusion of texts in the curriculum and about literary canon making. The question simply is: What is worthy of literary study and ought to be taught in the classroom?

The problem simply is that the syllabus is not a holdall. Every course can take only so many texts. No more! Today, thanks to advances in theory and alternative historiography such as the feminist and the subaltern, we can see that the traditional approach has been far from perfect. It has ignored the marginalised—the lower classes/castes, minorities, women, and ethnic groups—by excluding these from the canon.

The new thinking has been salutary for the teacher and the taught. For one thing, no longer can we swear in terms of "high" or "low" literature. Indeed, we now know that many texts traditionally disparaged as lowbrow exotica—crime and detective fiction, adventure narrative, gothic and the vampire story, the Westerns, and even erotica—can be read for pleasure and profit. So, Edgar Rice Burroughs' *Tarzan of the Ape* can tell us, as Leslie Fiedler so strikingly shows, about race relationships and the nightmarish anxiety of the white male about the "threat of the inter-racial rape."

For post-colonial societies like ours, that have both the unavoidable and unenviable task of dealing with English cultural history, there are many ways of responding to a problematic text other than a mere acceptance or rejection. We can, for instance, look at such texts as Harish Trivedi perceptively shows, through the prism of Indian and comparative literature. There will be many echoes of the Shakespeare debate this side of the Suez. We may not agree to an equal degree about the greatness of Shakespeare. There may be, similarly, two opinions regarding public funding of controversial plays and texts. But we must remember finally that texts are not good or bad in themselves, there are only ways of reading that are useful or banal.

The Burden of the Past
The ICHR Controversy

A mixed reaction seems to rule the ICHR controversy. While some fear misinterpretations, others feel that this will pave the way for writing the real history of India. The fluctuating image of the nation can be given shape by being more accommodative, argues the author.

The decision to reconstitute the Indian Council for Historical Research (ICHR) has unleashed a debate of near atavistic fury. The replacement of eighteen nominated members, part of the twenty-five member council, some fear, would sound the death knell of "objective and scientific history," paving the way for a majoritarian and exclusive interpretation of our past. Others view it as an attempt to rectify a disciplinary wrong, to write the "real" history of India. Yet, many issues go beyond the present debate between the Marxist and Nationalist historians and call for a careful consideration.

These problems could be articulated by a series of questions—How do we determine our individual and collective self-image? How is the question of our identity formation linked with our view of the past? How much of the memory of our past shall we retain, and how much of the trauma and nightmare abandon? How does the Jewish identity, for instance, deal with exile and holocaust, the Black American with the experience of slavery, or the Hindu psyche with the Islamic presence? "History," says Ronald Takaki, "is power. Society's collective memory determines the future. The battle is over what should be remembered and who should do the remembering."

At one level, the battle over Indian historiography is the fight between rival approaches and rival narratives of the past—economic versus political, "material" versus "spiritual," the chronicle of empires versus the history of agrarian relations, history from below versus the history of the ruling classes.

More significantly, the issue revolves around the central meaning we attach to the notion of the nation and nationality. Is India a timeless, eternal being, a spirit and soul, as some like Bankim or Sri Aurobindo believe? Can it be identified, as others advocate, with certain traditions, cultures and ways of belief? Or is the Indian nation a historically constructed category, "an imagined community," as Benedict Anderson terms it? Its greatness might deny what Partha Chatterjee calls its "fragments." Is the meaning of India, then, to be found in its master narratives, the great epics and scriptures of the classical tradition? Or does it lie in the innumerable little traditions, the folk, the tribal, the dalit and the marginal? Is India a cohesive cultural reality or is it only a coalition of interests? Clearly, the answer would depend on one's location and vantage point.

The debate over the centre and the periphery is not peculiar to India alone. Similar debates have surfaced in recent times elsewhere as well. In the U.S., for instance, literary critic Allan Bloom in his *Closing of the American Mind* (1990) laments the national neglect of the European classics, Plato and Homer in particular. These texts, he contends, are seminal; they provide the bedrock to American civilisation. Similarly, conservative critic E.D. Hirsch, in his *Cultural Literacy: What Every American Ought to Know* (1987), regrets that the American young lack the basic knowledge of their culture. "To be culturally literate," argues Hirsch, "is to possess the basic information needed to thrive in the modern world."

Is history, then, meant for restoring cultural pride? Is it merely a tool for political empowerment? Is Afro-centrism the answer to a Eurocentric view of history and culture? Some would think so. For instance, *Black Athena*, written from the Afro-centric point of view, argues that Western civilisation arose not in Greece or Rome but in Egypt and Africa. On the other hand, in 1988, for instance, William Bennett, conservative secretary of education in the U.S., debated on national television with the President of Stanford University. It was on whether traditional intellectual qualities represented by the so-called classics of literature such as *Iliad*, *The Republic* and Shakespeare's plays should give way to texts like Simone de Beauvoir's *Second Sex*, with their overriding concern with social values of equality of gender and race. Similarly, Dinesh D'Souza, in his *Illiberal Education*, questions some of the assumptions of currently accepted multicultural education.

If all social phenomenon are a complex affair and heterogeneity the hallmark of social living, then why must all critics and approaches be grouped into the simplistic categories of the Left or the Right? Marxist and subaltern historians like Romila Thapar, Sumit Sarkar and Ranajit Guha have clearly illumined our understanding of the material conditions we live in, of social fractures and fault lines. They have questioned monolithic models of nation building that see virtue in cohesion and all-effacing commonality. But why must we assume that all non-Marxist interpretation will be blind or will automatically be impervious to democratic, egalitarian drives?

The past will be a burden only if we have blinkers on. Only the doctrinaire can make the apriori rejection of the historicity of mythical characters, just as the equally blind votaries of cultural nationalism define India in narrow sectarian terms.

Today, new ways of looking at literary history have led to salutary results. They question, as Leslie Fiedler shows in *What Was Literature*, the categories of the so-called Major and Minor Author Tradition, the notions of the Classic and Popular Literature. In America, for instance, new anthologies such as the Heath and Norton, record the literary, cultural experience of diverse, hitherto marginalised groups—American Indians, Spanish explorers, French settlers, slave spirituals, folk ballads of Mexican Americans, as well as early feminist manifestos. As Russell

Reising aptly observes: This is one significant expression of our "usable past."

There will always be the burden of the past upon us. Our image of the self, the community, and the nation forever fluctuates. We can hope to give shape to this image, to a larger and more accommodative vision of the nation only through a spirit of dialogue, what Patrick J. Hill calls "a conversation of respect" to all rival points of view rather than through mutual hostility, confrontation or condemnation. Only then can we serve the interests of history and make the past a source of strength.

Dreaming Indian: Acting as Writer?: The Importance of Regional Languages

The question is no longer whether an Indian can write creatively in English, but what function he or she performs by so doing.

Somewhere in our worthy land, a lower middle class family agonised about the future of their only child, handicapped by a congenital defect in speech and hearing. After prolonged treatment, there was a ray of hope. "A cure is possible," said the doctors. But there was a catch. "The child can handle only one language." The response of the parents and the whole family was immediate and unanimous: of course, the language had to be English! *None* of the family members spoke the language, *not one* in their community knew it. Yet they thought nothing of foisting a language in such an insensitive manner and in condemning a child to a lifelong cultural alienation.

The parents were wise, English is the manna from Heaven, the passport to all success. And English it had to be!

Apocryphal? This incredible real-life story was movingly narrated by Professor U.R. Ananthamurthy, President of the Sahitya Akademi at the National Colloquium of Young Writers and Poets at the India International Centre, New Delhi. To an audience that comprised virtually every major language group of the land, Ananthamurthy's question was deeply disturbing. Yet, as a fellow delegate and speaker at the same colloquium, I find it hard to share the perception of my friend, Vijay Nambisan, in his account of the debate (*The Hindu*, 21 March 1993). I am sorry Nambisan has termed the issue one of "demagogy," "populism," and "linguistic fundamentalism." My essay is not a report of the colloquium, nor is it a defence of Ananthamurthy or the Sahitya Akademi. I shall, therefore, let the details—who said what—pass, and reformulate the problem in my own way.

Contrary to what Nambisan claims, the issue in question is not whether one can write creatively in English or not. Indeed, at the colloquium were present several talented Indian writers in English like Bapsi Sidhwa, Kavery Bhatt, Makarand Paranjape, and Vijay Nambisan himself. There was also a special session chaired by Upamanyu Chatterjee. These are ample proof, if proof were needed, that the issue is conclusively settled. The questions rather are—What is the relationship between the literary creativity of the Indian writer in English and the Indian tradition? What is the nexus between language, culture and hegemony? What role does literature play vis-à-vis cultural elitism and democratic pluralism? And finally, what function has the English-speaking intelligentsia in this country served in widening the gap between what Leavis called "mass civilisation" and "minority culture?" (One of the consequences of such a gap, I maintain, is the tragedy of Ayodhya and the rise of religious fundamentalism.)

On the other hand, the more limited question of the ethics of writing in English has been debated from Buddhadev Bose, P. Lal, David McCutcheon and Raja Rao onwards. Do write creatively in English, if you can turn it into a language of gossip, dream or the kitchen, as Ananthamurthy declared. The world of the Super Powers, diplomacy, international business and media, as well as language battles within the country constantly tell us of the importance of English as a link language or a language of communication. But even a creative writer in English has to locate himself in a milieu and has to respond to a living tradition—the world of myths, legends, folklore, rituals, metaphors and archetypes accessible to a large section of his audience. Surely an Indian English writer can accomplish this task. But has he? How far has he succeeded? What are the facts?

No one need invoke Edward Said's *Orientalism* (1978) or Antonio Gramsci's *Prison Notebook* to speak of the unabashed manner in which the English-speaking intelligentsia (with honourable exceptions) in this country has promoted for forty years a self-validating coterie-culture with one eye constantly turned towards the West for approval. Easy access to the publishing industry, the institutional network and the media have always lent a disproportionate space to the English-educated elite, whereas the thousands of our regional writers in countless provincial towns have continued to languish for want of outlet and/or patronage. Even the more successful of them find it hard to break out of their cultural zones.

Which is why listening to poets like Kumar Ambuj, Chandra Prakash Deval, Sukumaran, Pravasini Mahakud, Rajani Purulkar and other poets at the colloquium was an educative experience and a privilege. Kannada poet H.S. Shivaprakash spoke eloquently of Allama Prabhu, of the Vachana tradition, his penchant for the mythical world, "the frequent visits to the forgotten and marginalised regions of the past," his creative encounter with the poetry of Muktibodh, Aktar-ul-Iman, or of Ramakant Rath, Satchidanandan, Amitabh Gupta, Vinaychandran, Bharat Naik, Kunji Patel . . .

Yet, how many of us English-educated writers, poets and critics know of such creative writing and the rich traditions they represent? How threatened do we feel when even occasionally a quasi-Government body like the Sahitya Akademi brings our "regional writers" together and allows them to voice their anguish, indignation and anger at being sidelined?

Finally, the question of our accountability to our milieu and society. I am not berating the Indian-English writer for failing to respond to the Ayodhya crisis. Nor am I suggesting that the next poem that Rukmini Bhaya Nair or Nambisan writes ought to focus on the headline of the previous day. Such a demand for artistic commitment is both crude and specious. What I am suggesting instead is that the relationship between the creative artist—Indian-English or otherwise—and his/her native tradition that is complex, heterogenous and pluralistic, constantly fluid and evolving, is an important ongoing process. It makes possible works like Ramachandra Gandhi's *Sita's Kitchen* that emerge out of our deep dialogue with the past.

We can dismiss the concerns of the majority—their spiritual needs as obscurantism or their search for social justice as "mandalism" only at our own peril. Creativity and culture are not ivory tower concepts, but must be ultimately related to the life of the people and the nation. Giving more space to our many languages and pluralistic traditions is not an act of charity, but *the only way* English language and the English-speaking class can survive in this land.

These, as I see, are some of the logical corollaries to the question Ananthamurthy posed—our mindless craze for the latest MTV show and the latest frolic of Madonna, the systematic denial and denigration of our regional languages, and the way we valorise a hierarchy of cultures; the honorific distinctions made between "regional press" of the vernaculars and the English language "national press."

We can write in English or in any Indian language. That's not the point in issue. Indeed, the nest of our Indian-English writers, as Vikram Seth remarked in a recent interview, are "extremely mixed beasts." But there are larger questions that we need to ponder over. What is the Indian writer's place in his cultural milieu? What accounts for his irrelevance in the upheavals of the land? Finally and tragically, what explains our death wish to create a generation of clones, as Ananthamurthy's account quoted at the beginning so instructively revealed? It is to these questions that we need to turn. The task is no doubt formidable. But as Basavanna so aptly said:

Darkness is immense
So can you say, "The lamp is too small?"
No, Sir. You must not.

The Social Vision of Sri Aurobindo

15 August happens to be Sri Aurobindo's birthday, the day India attained its freedom. Sri Aurobindo did not regard the event as a fortuitous coincidence but as a divine dispensation. On the occasion of the fiftieth anniversary of Indian Independence and the hundred-and-twenty-fifth birthday of Sri Aurobindo, I take a closer look at the lesser known aspect of Sri Aurobindo's political legacy to India and the world.

The traditional view of Sri Aurobindo is that he was a poet and mystic who propounded the theory of creative evolution, the system of integral yoga, and established an ashram in the south of India. Romain Rolland called him the greatest synthesis between the East and the West. Aldous Huxley nominated him for the Nobel Prize for Literature. Rabindranath Tagore treated him as a leader. To his followers, Sri Aurobindo was an *avatar* who envisioned a new millennium, the coming of a new race, a new species of humanity whose guiding principle would not be the fractured human kind but what he termed in *The Life Divine* the Supermind or the Gnostic Consciousness. His detractors, however, find fault with Sri Aurobindo's retreat from political action to the life of a spiritual recluse.

Both the groups, however, see Sri Aurobindo as conveniently closeted within the domain of the "spiritual." To most of our countrymen, "the spiritual" evokes otherworldly concerns, matters of our soul rather than of the world. Thus, we think of Sri Aurobindo as we think of the Buddha, Mahavira, Adi Shankara, Vivekananda, Ramakrishna and Ramana Maharshi. It is rarely that we associate any of these figures with the mundane.

Take Sri Aurobindo, for instance. For the most part of the life, he remained committed to the fate of India and the world. This covers his fiery Bande Mataram days (1905-1910), imprisonment in the Alipore Jail, his concern over the fate of World War II and opposition to Nazism, the Cripps Mission to India, and the Independence Day message in 1947 (in which he warned of civil strife in and foreign invasions of a severely weakened and truncated India), his message during the Korean War and his opposition to Stalinism. During his political exile in Pondicherry, Sri Aurobindo spoke his mind on national and international issues to visitors, among whom were Devdas Gandhi, Lajpat Rai, Purushandas Tandon, and C.R. Das. He even sent an emissary when Sir Stafford Cripps visited India on his mission.

At least two separate efforts were made by the nationalists, who invited Sri Aurobindo during his Pondicherry phase, to join active politics. One was by Joseph Baptista, who offered editorship of an English daily, to be brought out from Bombay as the organ of a new political party under the leadership of Tilak and others. The other was by Dr. Munje, a Congress leader of Nagpur, who met Sri Aurobindo and invited him to take up the Presidentship of the Indian National Congress. To Baptista, Sri Aurobindo said that he himself must be "internally armed and equipped for my work before I leave it." Though he was in his "cave of Tapasya," Sri Aurobindo declared that he "does not at all look down on politics or political action." He went on to say:

> I have always laid a dominant stress and I now lay an entire stress on the spiritual life, but my idea of spirituality has nothing to do with ascetic withdrawal or contempt or disgust of secular things. There is nothing secular, all human activity is for me a thing to be included in a complete spiritual life, and the importance of politics at the present time is very great. But my line and intention of political activity would differ considerably from anything now current in the field. . . . What preoccupies me now is the question: what it [India] is going to do with its self-determination,

> how will it use its freedom, on what lines is it going to determine its future . . .?

Maintaining that he was a believer in the ideal of social democracy that Baptista's party believed in, Sri Aurobindo said it was "not in any of the form now current," and that he was not "altogether in love with the European kind." He stated: "India, having a spirit of her own and a governing temperament and proper to her own civilisation, should in politics as in everything else, strike out her own original path and not stumble in the wake of Europe." Similarly, in a letter dated 30 August 1920 to an admirer, Sri Aurobindo outlined the conflicting views he had vis-à-vis the Congress leadership, its philosophy, and programme of action. He concluded:

> The central reason, however, is that I am no longer first and foremost a politician but have definitely commenced another kind of work with a spiritual basis, a work of cultural and economic reconstruction of an almost revolutionary kind and an even making or at least supervising a sort of practical or laboratory experiment in that sense which needs all the attention and energy that I can spare.

The same sentiment was expressed in Sri Aurobindo's letter to Barindra Kumar Ghose, his younger brother. In a message dated 1 December 1922, Sri Aurobindo spelt out his approach:

> I do not believe that the Mahatma's principle can be the true foundation or his programme the true means of bringing out the genuine freedom and greatness of India, her Swarajya and Samrajya. On the other hand, others would think that I was sticking to the school of Tilakite nationalism. That also is not the fact. . . . I hold that school to be out of date. My own policy, if I were in the field, would be radically different in principle and programme from both, however it might coincide in certain points.

Those who are concerned about the grave crisis in India today should read two essays by Sri Aurobindo—"The Unhindu Spirit of Caste Rigidity" and "The Hindu Sabha." For here, we find answers to two of the crucial problems—cultural nationalism and social injustice. In one, Sri Aurobindo affirms the baleful influence of caste stratification and the need for democratic power-sharing. And in the other, he rejects the action of Hindu nationalism on modern lines. "We do not understand Hindu nationalism as a possibility under modern conditions," he says. His answer is clear. Though largely Hindu, it has to be a nationalism that is plural and composite, and encompasses all the cultural and religious strands of the land.

It is true that Sri Aurobindo spearheaded, during the freedom struggle, the Bengali religious nationalism. Like Bipin Chandra and Vivekananda, he believed in the relevance of the cultural and civilisational missions of India to the world. But he had nothing to do with the Hindu Right. As Sri Aurobindo put it vividly: "Recover the source of all strength in yourselves and all else would be added to you—social soundness, intellectual preeminence, political freedom, the mastery of human thought." The primacy that he sought was not for hegemony or dominance but what Partha Chatterji would aptly term one of "the two forms of anti-colonial nationalism, one outer and material, the other inner and spiritual." As Chatterji explains, the imitation of the coloniser by the subject nation exposes the nationalistic endeavour to the loss of "the distinctive spiritual essence of the national culture."

Regarding the Hindu-Muslim problem, Sri Aurobindo had this to say:

> Hindu-Mahomedan unity cannot be effected by political adjustments or Congress . . . It must be sought deeper down in the heart and in the mind, for where the causes of disunion are, there the remedies must be sought. As a political question, the Hindu-Mahomedan problem does not interest us at all; as a national problem, it is of supreme importance.

It is clear, therefore, that though committed to a spiritual view of India and the world's future, a political understanding of national and international affairs was integral to Sri Aurobindo's thinking. In laying stress on the primacy of inner change, Sri Aurobindo did not exclude the importance of external action. He constantly emphasised diversity, on federalism and confederalism, self-determination and freedom as the key principles of human progress. Much before ethnicity became a watchword, Sri Aurobindo saw the crucial role that language, culture and ideology played in the collective domain. In his message to the Andhra University in 1948, for instance, Sri Aurobindo spoke of the importance of India's regional cultures.

At the international level, he spoke of the need to democratise the U.N. Security Council, prophesised that communism, of the Bolshevist kind would not remain a monolith, and that certain forms of it might even take the shape of cooperative socialism, more in keeping with the freedom of the individual and the ultimate realisation of human unity.

These were some of the seed-ideas and founding principles of Sri Aurobindo's political philosophy. Many of them have already been realised. Today, liberation of India and Asia is an accomplished fact. And we are inexorably heading towards the actualisation of the rest. As we are celebrating the fiftieth anniversary of India's Independence that coincides with Sri Aurobindo's birthday on 15 August, we shall do well to salute Sri Aurobindo and his political legacy for the building of modern India.

"Feminism Must Reach out to the World"

Sandra Gilbert, one of the leading literary feminists of the world, talks about her path-breaking work, the challenges before contemporary feminism—East and West, her poetry, and human relationships in general.

Sandra Gilbert would easily rank as one of the most outstanding literary feminists writing today. Noted for her pioneering work, *The Mad Woman in the Attic* (Cornell, 1973), co-authored by Susan Gubar, Professor Gilbert began her career by charting out a path-breaking study of the woman writer and the nineteenth century literary imagination. Other achievements soon followed—*Shakespeare's Sisters: Feminist Essays on Women Poets* with Gubar (IU, 1979), *The Norton Anthology of Literature by Women: The Tradition in English* with Gubar (Norton, 1985), *No Man's Land: The Place of the Woman Writer in the Twentieth Century* (Yale, 1987), and many others.

Sandra Gilbert is also a poet of rare distinction. She has seven collections of poems to her credit. In addition, she has a memoir *Wrongful Death: A Medical Tragedy* (Norton, 1995) and a critical account of poetry called *Acts of Attention: The Poems of D.H. Lawrence* (Cornell, 1973). Her forthcoming book is *Inventions of Farewell: A Millennial Book of Elegies* (Norton, 2000). Sandra Gilbert teaches at the University of California, Davis.

Recently on a visit to India, her first such trip, Professor Gilbert flew in from Chennai to address the Annual MELUS (Multi-Ethnic Literatures of the United States) Conference at the ASRC (Now IACIS), Hyderabad. Next day, a friend, Sukalpa, and I met her at the Krishna Oberoi. It was a bright day. Sandra

Gilbert looked resplendent as she sat facing us and the sunlight filtered through the glass panes. From the fifth floor window, we could see the shimmering waters of Hussain Sagar Lake.

Excerpts from the Interview

SM: You are generally known for your pivotal work *Madwoman in the Attic*. This is about female imagination in nineteenth century literature. What prompted you to write this book in the first place, and what cultural and ideological factors were responsible for the way it was received?

SG: Well, Susan Gubar and I began teaching at the Indiana University in the Fall of 1973. We met in the elevator one day. We were rather lonely then because we were new in town, and we became good friends. Susan thought that it would be good for us to teach a course together. That would make our life a little easier! The Department wanted a course in Literature by Women. That was not really our field. Susan was working on the Eighteenth Century, and I had just published my first book, *Acts of Attention: The Poetry of D.H. Lawrence*. There was a complete readjustment in our intellectual lives. We were very interested in teaching this course. So we just found our way into this field; completely taught ourselves because there were no courses in literature by women at that time. We argued a lot about what we were going to call the course. I wanted to call it "Upstairs, downstairs" after a TV programme. Susan thought that was quite vulgar. And I said, "What about 'Mad Woman in the Attic'?" because I was haunted by the metaphors of female imagination in *Jane Eyre*. And so, we started with that book. Then we began to build a syllabus, built up a reading list. We basically put together a list of all the writings of women we knew, some that we did not know. We wanted to see what happens when we read them in juxtaposition with each other. So, if you read Emily Dickinson with Ralph Waldo Emerson along with Thoreau or Whitman, then what happens? What happens if you read Mary Shelley along with Emily Dickinson and later on Sylvia Plath? And so that was what we basically did. We put all the texts together, and we were overwhelmed by what happened. It turned out that there were all these connections between these texts, all kinds of parallels, all kinds of echoes, all kinds of images carried over and over again, which were common to women writers in the nineteenth century. From weeks after starting this class, we knew that we had to write a book about it. We were just seized by the book and wrote it in white heat, to quote Emily Dickinson. It got published quite rapidly and was very well received.

To turn to the second part of your question, this was a time when the Women's Movement in the United States was really building; it was full of energy and excitement. There were consciousness-raising groups throughout the country. Everyone was experiencing the second wave of the feminist movement, and there had not been many books before. We knew of Elaine Showalter's work; my husband had been a reader of her book at the University of California at Davids where she got her PhD, and we knew a few other people who were doing the kind of work that we were doing. We were very fortunate because we were writing at an originatory moment, a moment people were looking at the way female imagination responded to pressures and oppressions of patriarchal culture. I think that was one reason why the book was so well received, and we were lucky indeed.

SM: Despite the importance of this book, do you at times feel irritated to be identified as a single book celebrity? Salinger's *Catcher in the Rye* type of author?

SG: Of course I do!

SM: Yesterday again, you were introduced by Amritjit Singh as a writer of a path-breaking . . .

SG: Since the first book, we have produced a three-volume sequel. We hoped that in many ways, we had learnt from all the mistakes made earlier, to be more sophisticated and more advanced. I don't know whether in the long view of history, I would be happy to be identified as the author of a book that was influential and that made a difference to people. It's presumptuous, crude, and rude to complain! Nonetheless, it is true that we have done a lot of other work, including the *Norton Anthology of Literature by Women*.

SM: Professor Gilbert, one finds in your work an element of sympathy in your critical judgement. Is it because you are a creative writer that you eschew dogmatism in ideological matters?

SG: Well, I can't be sure of that! I hope so! I do look at things from the point of view of a writer. I write as an artist, and I like to think that my work as a critic is enriched by my work as a poet.

SM: I was coming to that! Do you think that your work as a critic hampers your creative writing, or is it the other way around?

SG: My answer to that question always has been, "Well, certainly not." If anything, my two worlds feed each other and energise each other!

SM: Matthew Arnold's Function of Criticism at the Present Time?

SG: Yes. I'd like to think that there is a fruitful reciprocity between my work as a poet and my work as a critic. But you know, one day I realised, "Well, how can you know?" How can I know what kind of poetry I'd have written if I had not been working as a critic!

SM: How would you describe yourself as a feminist? As a liberal, socialist, Marxist, or free-thinker?

SG: I am a very passionate, very committed feminist. I worry that the feminist movement has not gone ahead. I guess all political movements have their moments of backsliding and deal with a kind of backlash that Susan Faludi has written about.

SM: I'll come to that presently!

SG: As I said yesterday, fundamentally I am a kind of psychoanalytical feminist. I don't want to discount cultural issues or issues of class or race that are focussed into analysis by Marxist feminists. But my intention is tc think that there are transcultural realities that oppress or subordinate all women. This is not to discount all of the other things that determine how a woman deals with her femininity. But that is something that I think women have in common with each other, all over the world, and I think it is important for feminists to remember that!

SM: What, according to you, are the main challenges before feminism at the beginning of the next millennium?

SG: I think the main challenge faced by feminism within the academy, which is where I am, is to reach out beyond the academy to people, to regular people in the streets and the world. I think there has been a tendency for feminism in the academy, certainly in the United States, to become very ingrown, very specialised. I try to write so that my mother, who is 96 years old and lives at Jackson Heights, and my daughters who are not academics, understand what I have to say.

SM: Some detractors maintain that it is not easy for hard-boiled feminists to celebrate femininity and the world of love which believe in mutual dependence. What do you think?

SG: Certainly, a valid question! Somebody asked me this at Chennai. Do feminists repudiate femininity? I mean, I have a counter question. What is femininity? What is the feminine? Feminism asks these questions. But does it mean that values associated cross-culturally with maternal nurture, with love, generosity and charity, or with friendship, are repudiated? There is no feminist caveat that I know of that forbids that sort of thing!

SM: Why is it that this misconception has persisted at the popular level for so long?

SG: It is probably part of the backlash against feminism. The depiction of feminists as wild-eyed, rabid rabble-rousers goes back to some of the response to Mary Wollstonecraft. All because she asked for rights for women and she wrote about women's rights.

SM: One often hears of feminist backlash typified by works of critics like Susan Faludi. What are your views regarding this backlash? Why is the backlash taking place now? All over the world, one finds, for instance, an upsurge of orthodoxy, fundamentalism, and the emergence of the Right. Do you think these have something to do with the backlash?

SG: There are so many factors that are responsible for the phenomenon that it is hard to determine what really causes this backlash. The issue of global fundamentalism is one I am prepared to address. However, it will require an analyst far more sophisticated than I am to address this issue. On the other hand, the kind of backlash that feminists have encountered can be traced back to the time when women began to enter at the turn of the century to the public sphere both in the United States and England. I think here in India it probably did not happen until later. When women began to enter higher education and enter the professions, naturally there were men who did not wish to give up their places to women. They did not wish to share. They were afraid that they would lose their position of power which they had enjoyed in the last. It is like a child saying, "you can't have my toy, you can't have part of my playground, you can't have my cookies, you can't have my biscuit or muffin!"

SM: Many feel that while the woman in our country has emerged as a strong and self-reliant being, discovering and realising the many dimensions of her personality, a corresponding evolution is not seen in the Indian male, most of whom remain mamma's boys, incapable of having relationships with strong, individualised women. Do you think most American men remain mama's boys?

SG: I think a lot of American men are either dependent on mothers or they have to distance themselves from their mothers by being macho, which is just another side of the same coin. But I think you are asking a question that is very nuanced—What happens in developing countries and what happens to relationships in such a context. One may argue that such relationships are influenced, as the people in Subaltern Studies have suggested, by the relationship between such countries and colonial powers. This, of course, will take a long time to study [laughs].

SM: What do you think should be done in order to take feminism to the wider world, apart from the need to talk to the common people and use a language that is intelligible?

SG: What I've been seeing in India has deeply impressed me. For instance, I have watched in the Indian media many feminists who are advocating strong female role models and women who have relationships of equality within families.

SM: Why do you think many women admit to being interested in women's issues but refuse to be labelled as feminists? Do you think that they are trying to send a message regarding themselves because of societal pressures? What is it?

SG: Susan Gubar and I call this syndrome "I am not a feminist but . . . !" You know, at the beginning of our course on Literature by Women that we organised, we went around the table and heard several women say: "I am not a feminist *but* I do believe in equal pay for equal work, I do believe in co-parenting. . . ." It turned out that they believed in everything that feminism stood for, but they did not wish to be defined as feminists. And so, feminism becomes a kind of dirty word: "I am not a bitch, but . . . !"

SM: You have written a fine admiring book on the poetry of D.H. Lawrence. Did it require courage to admire Lawrence when he had been perceived, especially in your times, as a bate-noir by many feminists?

SG: I get asked that question a lot. I felt one time that it was an embarrassment to be a Lawrence admirer. As a feminist, I realise that there are many misogynistic ideas in Lawrence. However, I also realise that the power of Lawrence is great precisely because he has a direct pipeline to the cultural unconscious. He is completely, unswervingly and unashamedly an honest writer. His honesty is such that he is willing to admit to things that a lot of his male contemporaries would not admit to. He is willing to say things that are scandalous and embarrassing. I have to admire him for that! He does say misogynistic things, but when he does so, he is in effect acting out most of his anxieties that we have been talking about!

SM: Your current work is a cultural study of widowhood, as a sequel to an elegy you wrote called "Wrongful Death," the inexplicable death of your husband, who also taught English Literature at the University of California at Davis. How would you theorise grief? I recall what you said yesterday, that patterns of grief are found across cultures and are socially constructed.

SG: Well, I have begun thinking about that. These are very preliminary and provisional ideas. My book is going to be about the poetry of grief in general and not just about widowhood. I am very much influenced by the view that women seem to be the ones who do the most passionate and direct lamenting within the context of grief, while men do the public eulogy. Probably it has something to do with the fact that men, as mama's boys, have to be public creatures who display their masculinity through a kind of stylised and ceremonial grief.

SM: What is your book *The Fourth World* about? Is it, as my friend Sukalpa says, about gendered indigenous space?

SG: You know, I had not looked at it that way! I have always been looking for a metaphor away from all the three worlds we know. That's the realm of art, the realm of fantasy, imagination, and so on. I call that the fourth world! I discover that in the native American myth, the world of the Navajo, the visionary world.

SM: Lawrence often refers to this world as the fourth dimension as in his collection *The Death of the Porcupine and Other Essays.*

SG: Yes, that's right!

SM: What is your assessment of the contribution of Indian feminism?

SG: Well, Indian feminists have been very strong, very important in a whole range of ways. there are many Indian feminists who have recently addressed the issue of Sati, and I have read a lot written by Indian feminists. There are also many important aspects of Indian feminism that are manifested in the West through the writings of Gayatri Chakravorty Spivak. Although she attacked our reading of *Jane Eyre*, we welcome her comments and her contributions.

SM: And finally, what are your impressions of your visit to India? We understand it's your first visit.

SG: Yes, it's my first visit. All my life, I have wanted to come to India, and I am delighted that I am finally here!

Freedom and the Indian Diaspora

"Writing makes up a shelter and allows space to what would otherwise be hidden, crossed out and mutilated," said Indian-English poet Meena Alexander in her novel "The Shock of the Arrival." In an interview with the author, while on a visit to Hyderabad, the poet dwells on this point while discussing the post-colonial experience in America, romanticism, creative writing, and the cultural landscape of Kerala as an influence on her writings.

Meena Alexander is a well-known Indian-English poet. She lives in New York and works both at Hunter College and the Graduate Centre of the City University of New York where she is Professor of English and Creative Writing. Her work has featured widely in India, the United States and English, and has been translated into several languages including Italian and German. She has many collections of poetry, fiction and non-fiction to her credit. They include *The Storm* (1989), *Night Scene, The Garden* (a long poem that was produced off-Broadway in 1988), a novel *Nampally Road* (1991), *A House of Thousand Doors* (1988), *The River and Bridge* (1996), *The Shock of Arrival* (1996), and her recent novel *Manhattan Music* (1997).

Talking about the art of writing, Meena said in *The Shock of Arrival*: "Writing makes up a shelter, allows space to what would otherwise be hidden, crossed out and mutilated. Sometimes, writing can work towards a reparation, making a sheltering space for the mind. Yet it feeds off ruptures, tears in what might otherwise seem a seamless, oppressive fabric."

Meena Alexander carries her many distinctions lightly on her shoulders. She is sought after by poetry-reading groups on both sides of the Atlantic as well as in India. One of her early poems was published, she recalls, when she was a lecturer at the Central Institute of English and Foreign Languages, Hyderabad. It was about a room in a state of disrepair. Following the publication of the poem in *The Critical Quarterly*, the Director of the CIEFL paid her a visit to enquire if she was satisfied with her accommodation. He thought the poem was about campus housing and could mean bad publicity internationally for the Institute. That is the majority view of poetry, Meena said with a laugh as we sat down at the CIEFL campus to discuss her views on fiction, post-coloniality, and the experience of the Indian diaspora.

Excerpts from the Interview

SM: In popular imagination, the "post-colonial" has often come to mean the Third World and the diaspora. How would you define the "post-colonial" experience in an advanced country like the U.S., taking yourself as an example?

MA: I think the word "post-colonial" is relevant not just to a country like India (which has celebrated its fiftieth anniversary in 1999), it is also extremely relevant to countries like the U.S. where the issue of a multicultural nation is not just hotly debated but is a reality. In fact, in terms of the demography, roughly by 2010 A.D., the majority of Americans would become the so-called minority, i.e., Asians, African-Americans, Latinos, etc. What it really means is that there is, within the U.S., a population that has emigrated because the country is built on layer upon layer of migrants from the erstwhile Third World. Even within New York city, you will find whole neighbourhoods that are not Anglo-Americans, they are not White. Now the question of "post-colonial" in the U.S. has different connotations, obviously a different meaning than it has in India or the Indian diaspora.

Perhaps what we really mean by the term is the fabrication of a particular kind of knowledge within which there exists a tension between the newness of what is being made and an older way that may be covered over or masked, which resisted that emergence. You know, I have this book called *The Shock of Arrival*, and it was my editor who insisted on a subtitle, *Reflections on the Post-Colonial Experience*. Well, obviously it is not a general, a sort of blanket statement. Each experience is different.

After my novel *Manhattan Music* came out, this young woman came. She is a Uzbeki from Afghanistan. And she had travelled from Afghanistan to Pakistan to Saudi Arabia to London. Finally she came to New York. And she said to me: "Your novel *Manhattan Music* speaks to me; it is a post-colonial novel." And I said: "What do you mean by 'post-colonial'?" And she said: "Well, I have gone to a lot of places, and the novel is about somebody who is moving. Now, does 'post-colonial' mean somebody who is moving?" It does not, not necessarily! The idea of a shifting frame of reference, of multiple worlds, these often are part of the post-colonial knowledge, but these don't have to be. India is currently a post-colonial society, but then, of course, there are people whom post-colonialism have never touched. In fact, it is totally irrelevant to their experience. So, is their experience "post-colonial?" Well, I don't know. In many ways, "post-colonial" is relevant after the creation of the nation-state.

SM: Despite being a successful Indian-English poet, have you ever felt handicapped by the fact that you do not write in Malayalam, your mother tongue? Has it made any difference to your creative writing in English?

MA: Well, it's true I don't read or write Malayalam, but people have sometimes felt that maybe the rhythm of my writing is drawn from Malayalam. It is a very powerful oral presence to me. In fact, in *The Shock of Arrival*, I reflect on this issue, what it means not to write in one's mother tongue. Obviously, if I was in Kerala, I would have been a writer, but I would have been a very different sort of writer.

SM: One finds that academia in the West is quite progressive. And yet the mainstream American society has its share of racism and other forms of bigotry. This must pose a dilemma. How does your art mediate between these two worlds?

MA: Well, maybe it does not mediate at all. I don't really have an answer for that because I write and I am grateful for anybody who reads it.

SM: But surely you deal with society and it must pose problems. Do you use art to resolve such problems?

MA: I write poems as a person who walks in the street, not just somebody who uses the library. And the experience of which I draw to write are the experiences that come from being in the ordinary world. Racism is a fact. The language that the academy uses, particularly the progressive language, does not necessarily have a place in one's ordinary life. I think in many of my poems, there is that tension present between whatever my private ultimate feeling might be and how they are seen by the social world. I think in large chunks of my writing, particularly in *The Shock of Arrival*, I reflect on this kind of complicated doubleness that comes into existence when you have to speak your personal, private voice and you are not quite sure who had to hear the language and what shape the language must take.

SM: Wouldn't it be interesting to speculate what the non-White immigrant, the man in the street, in New York City, for instance, must think of the "post-colonial" experience?

MA: I think for him the issue of endurance would be a matter of consequence. You know, you survive and you make place in a culture where you are surviving so that in a sense it is not a grassroot issue: what it might mean to have a culture as a minority, as an immigrant. And I think that some of the children of Indians who are born in America don't know India. India for them is just an idea. It is for them as much of a myth as Africa is to African-Americans. It is also an ethnic idea—the transformation of nationality into ethnicity.

In fact, in *Manhattan Music*, I have Draupadi who is this character who says: "Oh, I wish I was Dorothy and I wish I was a Caribbean!" She has never been to India. The country is an idea, a fantasy for her that makes up an imagined history. She feels guilty that she does not have a history. This is something, I think, that touches a great many Americans because the mainstream does not really allow you the transparency of a sense of past. You feel that you have to invent the past. That's where writers become useful because I think writers and artists in a way invent the stories by which they give us a little piece of mirror in which to see ourselves. In *Manhattan Music*, the novel opens with an image of an old man sitting on Nampally Road selling spectacles from a heap, and each of the pieces shifts and catches the light. This is seen by one of the characters sitting in New York . . .

SM: In another context, you talk about the fact that writing for an audience, conscious or unconscious, could be a distraction. It might amount to auto-censorship . . .

MA: I think it's true. I mean, I feel so.

SM: It could be dangerous too. And there are reasons as to why it could be dangerous. But at the same time, many writers also testify to the fact that the presence of an audience provides some kind of motivation. If you are going to rule out writing for an audience as one of the options, then where do you think the writer is going to get his motivation from?

MA: Well, when I write, I do not consciously think about the audience. There is absolutely no question that when the work is finished, there is a great longing for someone to read it. In fact, there are the two different parts of the same process. But if, when I am writing, someone is going to see it and judge it, I find that very difficult. I have to give myself the free scope, and once it is finished, it is my choice. I send it out to a magazine or a journal, or I prefer readings from it because you want to share it with others.

SM: So what you are saying is that during the creative act, you are oblivious of the presence of the reader?

MA: That's right! Exactly! Because I think there is a greater privacy that you need for composition.

SM: Let me take you to a slightly different area. After you wrote *Nampally Road*, I remember that in America in 1991 you told me that it was a political novel, and that writing a novel is more difficult in some sense than writing poetry. And yet, what prompted you to write another novel *Manhattan Music*? What kinds of linkages do you think exist between the two?

MA: Well, you know, it's a very interesting question because there is a whole section on *Manhattan Music* that is set on Nampally Road, Hyderabad, and what I did is that I have two characters. The first is Sandhya, who is this very ordinary housewife living in Hyderabad; she did not have a job or anything; she goes to New York. The other character, this photographer, Jay, is an interesting character. He lives in Hyderabad and is a wonderful photographer. He becomes well known. He takes photos during the riots against the Sikhs in 1984 in Delhi, Sultanpuri and so on, you know, riot and so forth. He is printed in *Life* magazine, and he is very well known. Then he goes off to Germany, and later to America. In the new land, he can't take photographs very well because he does not know how to frame the scene, how to capture it. He wraps up his camera in the silk saree his mother gave him, and he starts writing poems. And people say: "Why are you writing poems? Who's going to read your poems?" It's a trajectory he has carried from Hyderabad, from Nampally Road to New York. But something got stopped in him, his creativity got stuck.

SM: Do you think your memoir *Fault Lines* is somehow linked with your book *The Shock of Arrival*, thematically and ideologically? Do you think there are some kind of connections?

MA: It's an interesting question! Someone who has completed her PhD on my writings said she saw *The Shock of Arrival* almost as an extension of *Fault Lines*. I'd never thought of it that way! She has read it that way, and I suppose there is a connection.

SM: For a poet and an artist dealing with the cultural world, what does border crossing mean?

MA: I think that is something that happens all the time in my mind. That happens in order to exist, but also in order to create one has to cross a border, or "jump over a well."

SM: Now, that's interesting! What do you mean by "jumping over a well?"

MA: You know, when I went to England in 1995 at the invitation of the Arts Council's International Writers in Residence Programme, I gave readings in many places—in two maximum security prisons, and in community centres. I read out to groups of older citizens who had been thrown out from Uganda but who were illiterate in English, people who were marginalised in their communities because many of the older people who came from East Africa did not speak English. So you have to imagine this sort of strange talk—having by my side a translator who would translate what I read into Gujarati for the audience. It was a very small audience. The first time it went off very well. The translators were wonderful; they had read my works and had sort of absorbed it in a way. The next time I went, I had a very strange experience. I have written about it. I went into the room and there was this very unwilling translator. I think being a Gujarati, he had been pressed into the job, and did not know what to do. He was very patronising about the whole thing. "These women," he said, "had to read their gas meter and pay their medical bills."

I didn't say very much. I read a poem "Bloodline," and he refused to translate. Then I read a section from my memoir in which I imagine women in Kerala lifting up their sarees and jumping over wells. I read out that specific section from my book. When I read that article, I thought that it had touched the women. There was something more. It had come to me because as a child I had been brought up with the idea that it was quite dangerous to go near the well if you were a girl because girls fall in; they don't jump, they are not pushed, they just fall in. Also, there was always the idea that it was something shameful, some illicit sexuality that came in—so and so's daughter got pregnant and ended up in a well! I had looked into the well as a child and I was fascinated to see my own face staring back at me; I was haunted by this image when I was writing my memoir. And I thought, instead of jumping into the well, suppose the women jump over the well! And thus the phrase "Well jumped, women." The translator just looked at me and said, "I refuse to translate that." He was very shocked; I asked him the reason. He said, "Madam, these women should jump into the wells." Meaning that, they should really end their lives. So, this was a very disturbing presence to me. And I really felt that it made visible to me something that I was writing against. Normally, I move among people who don't think poetry is rubbish, who think like you. But, in fact, there are certain elements in society that are driving one to write. And I was in the presence of something like that, something visible to me again! And so far, the refusal of this translator was very shocking. It revealed something to me about the sources of my own creativity.

SM: Your fellow writer, Arundhati Roy from Kerala, has produced what many rate as a masterpiece, *The God of Small Things*. Kerala's cultural landscape is enormously rich, given the presence of many influences-the Syrian Christian, the Islamic, the orthodox Hindu presence, and in more recent times, the image of the Malayali on the move. As a writer, have you reflected on this legacy? Has it given richness of experience to your writing?

MA: Well, I think a lot of my work draws on the imagery I have from my childhood in Kerala. For instance, if you look at my poems in *The House of Thousand Doors*, or the long poem *The Storm*, written in five parts, you will see that the landscape is very important to me. And now I am starting a new series of poems from that landscape because, you see, Kerala is a coastal region. And the idea of diaspora and border crossing is a very old one in Kerala. You know, it's a very ancient idea in Indian thought and culture, that you go away from home in order to gain knowledge. So, the idea of exile is not a post-modern one. On the contrary, it is a very ancient one. If you look at the great mystic poets of the Sangam period, you know, in the canonical literature, many of them go on journeys. Look at Meerabai. In fact, I have been recently reading a lot of Meerabai. And I have written a poem called "Indian April," which is an elegy for Allen Ginsberg who died recently. I read out the poem at New Brunswick at the beginning of 1999, just before I came here [to India]. Ginsberg wrote his Indian journal in Rajasthan. So, I imagined Meerabai coming to New York City. What would it be like? Therefore, I think, this border crossings, these diaspora, were something not necessarily alien to what we think of as the complex fabric of Indian society, Indian culture. Location is very important. It's not just one thing, it's a multiplicity of layers. I think Kerala in that way is very interesting because it has a very rich heritage of many cultures—Hindus, Muslims, Christians, Jains. It has a strong tradition of the Nair community, as well as a strong women's movement. It has a high level of literacy. And so I think Kerala is quite an exciting place in many ways to come from, it is an unusual sort of place. And I always go back. Not just because of my parents, but I need to see the water, the trees, the sky. I need to see the monsoon again. I love the rain.

SM: Your prose in the novel and non-fictional works is quite similar to your poetry. It has a lyrical flow; it is full of rich imagery and metaphor. Has this been inevitable? Or is it a conscious act because poetry for the most part involves very compressed expression?

MA: Well, it certainly is not conscious! I don't think about how the prose is crafted, but I think when I read a piece of prose, several people say: "Oh! It must be a poem you're reading!" And I disagree. But I suppose in the ancient idea of Kavya, the distinction between poetry and prose does not exist. In fact, if you look at a text like *Kadambari*, it is part poetry, part prose.

SM: There is something I've always wanted to ask. Is there any connection between your interest in romanticism and the interest in "post-colonialism," or are these parallel interests?

MA: Well, it's an excellent question. I am now at the Graduate Centre [of the City University of New York], teaching a course for the PhD programme called "Romanticism and Post-Colonialism." I think there is little doubt that the Romantic concern with subjectivity has been enormously formative in my writing, and also indirectly elliptically in my thinking about what one calls post-coloniality, the idea of meanings that is disjunctive of the mainstream social experience, the notion of the primacy of memory for instance. All these are notions in romanticism.

I am going to attend an international symposium in Canada on *Female Life Writing* for the bicentennial of Mary Wollstonecraft and Mary Shelley. It is two hundred years since the death of Mary Wollstonecraft and the death of Mary Shelley.

SM: What are your current and future writing plans?

MA: I am starting a new series of poems. They deal with a house, with ancestral memory, and various specific locations. They are densely packed. Ideally, I'd like to call these poems *Water*. So, I suppose my ambition is to write a series of clear poems!

The Best Words in Their Best Order

In the modern world, the poet stands as a prophet who, with his language, is able to communicate. His work is an inner calling, an act of peace. Blake Morrison, leading British poet, who served as the poetry editor of the TLS *and* The Independent, *is today involved in bringing the younger generation of poets to the public, helping to give poetry a future, as it were. He spoke to me on the buoyant poetry scene, about poems in translation, and poetry as a therapeutic form.*

Blake Morrison, who served as the poetry and literary editor of *The Times Literary Supplement* and *The Independent*, is a leading poet of Britain today. He is best known as the co-editor (with Andrew Motion) of *The Penguin Book of Contemporary British Poetry*. Apart from poetry collections, he has done critical studies on The Movement and Seamus Heaney.

Blake Morrison has received many awards—Eric Gregory Award, 1980; Somerset Maugham Award, 1984; Dylan Thomas Memorial Prize, 1985; Non-fiction Prize, 1993; and J. R. Ackedey Prize for Autobiography, 1994. He was the Chairman of the Poetry Book Society (1984-87) and Fellow of the Royal Society of Literature (1992).

In this free-wheeling interview conducted in his book-lined study at Blackheath, London, Morrison talks about the poetry situation in Britain today, anthology preparation, and the position of the poet in today's world.

Excerpts from the Interview

SM: Let's begin at the beginning. How and when did you begin writing poetry?

BM: I began writing poetry as a teenager really, in school. I can remember being sent an exercise of writing a poem, and walking down to my local village church into the graveyard, trying to be inspired by the dead people lying around. But then, when I was slightly older, in my late teens, I simply wrote for myself. And although I didn't write so much at the University as an undergraduate, the habit was there and continued in my twenties.

SM: Though the experience of war has produced some great poetry, many poets have also felt a sense of powerlessness on account of widespread conflict and the experience of total war. They have, in fact, chosen the path of silence. Do you think that the poet today suffers from the same fate due to the impact of the all-pervasive techno-economic culture?

BM: I think it is a difficult time for the poet today. Perhaps it is always a difficult time for poets. But I am thinking of the idea of George Steiner, that after the Second World War, after the concentration camps, that perhaps silence is the inevitable response of the poet. I think we've moved into a different phase now where the threat to poets isn't the recent traumatic memory so much as simply that of competition of the mass media. Newspapers have always many words, and for the poet to find the still, small voice and regional feeling with all this rivalry from other media, it's obviously difficult. And I suspect that many poets who have been poets now become other things, including, you know, musicians, pop musicians and so forth. So, it is a difficult time.

SM: In very broad terms, how would you like to comment on the poetry scene in Britain today, in the nineties?

BM: Yes, having been gloomy a second ago, I'd say that it's a surprisingly buoyant scene. We have now here a great deal more performance of poetry than we used to have. That's one of the things that have happened. There have been many more readings around the country, sometimes formal ones within the University, but many many informal ones in pubs and clubs, and poets have got used to having to stand up and read from their works as well as to write for the page. That's been quite a vibrant aspect of the culture. There's a newspaper, *The Independent*, which prints poems everyday. There have been documentaries on television where good poets like Tony Harrison have made poetic documentaries. We have something called National Poetry Day, where the nation's poets give readings. It's usually some sort of a television programme. And, of course, you know, the publishing scene, although it's always hard-pressed, has survived. Publishers, especially some of the bigger publishers who used to publish, no longer do, but the biggest ones still do, including Faber and Faber. Meanwhile, one or two regional publishers have sprung up, like the Carcanet Press in Manchester, who are producing a lot of poetry, so against all the odds, it's still not bad.

SM: We know that all anthologies are difficult business; it involves the painful process of inclusion and exclusion, selecting texts that the editor thinks are worth preserving that will stand the test of time. What was your experience while preparing the Penguin anthology of contemporary poetry and how has the volume been received?

BM: We were helped by the fact that we had a simple, exciting message to take into the world. That is to say, when Andrew Motion and myself were preparing the book round about 1980, we felt we were bringing to the attention of the public a generation of poets who hadn't yet been anthologised very much, and we believed that at least one of those poets, Seamus Heaney, was a major poet who deserved a far wider audience. Not far behind him were very good poets like Tony Harrison, Douglas Dunn, James Fenton and others. And so, we had this sense of mission really, bringing a younger generation of poets to the public. Now, of course, it meant leaving out poets. And that is always difficult. I'd say there may have been five poets, six poets, and even ten poets we might have put in, as there were five to six poets we did put in and might not have done. But we felt we had to keep a fairly small sample, twenty; limit ourselves. And if we had more time, things would have changed; some of the poets included would have been different. But here it was, though difficult, the rewarding thing to do. The reception, well, there was a controversy because . . .

SM: Yes, I was coming to that. Let me raise the question regarding the reception. The Penguin collection that you edited has been attacked by some as not being sufficiently multicultural in approach, while the critics of the multicultural school argue that there is an increasing tendency to evaluate the aesthetic in favour of the political, for allocating space surely on grounds of race, sex and gender. There is that debate going on. How do you respond to this?

BM: This will take a long time to answer. And I am going to keep it brief. The issue, the multicultural issue, was not particularly alive in Britain in 1980. Andrew Motion and I were conscious of the gender issue to some extent. We had in the background anthologies of poetry published in this country since 1945 that had, say out of hundred poets, 96 or 94 men. We wanted a better balance of men and women, and we included five women poets out of twenty. Still only a quarter! It's not balanced, and I think the situation is rather different now because now there are at least as many good women poets coming through as there are men. The multicultural issue, well, there are one or two black, that is to say, West Indian in origin, Afro-Caribbean poets who might have been included, like John Eggard and James Berry. And I think if we had been doing anthologies two to three years later, we would have had more to choose from. Perhaps, to be honest, with a slightly more raised awareness of the issue involved, we'd probably have handled it differently. But in 1980, these were not as live issues as they are now. I slightly regret it. To be perfectly honest with you, if I had a chance to do this anthology again, I wouldn't be so narrow. There will be thirty or forty poets and not twenty, there would be a far better representation of women poets and a far more multi-ethnic field to the book. That's not out of political correctness. It's simply a reflection of something that has happened here in the last fifteen years, that a lot more poetry has come from groups who were previously marginalised by a white male literary establishment. But there you are. We were working in 1980. Things were different then.

SM: What was you experience at the meeting on contemporary British poets in India in 1996? Did you have an opportunity to interact with the Indian-English poets there?

BM: Yes, I did. I was impressed by the knowledge of contemporary British literature that some of the participants at the seminar at Lonavala showed. I was, of course, disappointed to hear that contemporary British Literature is not taught in many places in India. Of course, contemporary British Literature has to compete with all other literatures of the world. I don't think it should have some special advantage because of the old friendship or the old association with India. But I do think there is a lot of good work being done in this country at the moment. I just like to feel that Indian professors who are interested in British Literature have moved on a bit from C.P. Snow, Graham Greene and so on, and were reading the contemporaries. But there you are, I know how difficult it is. I know how short of time they are, and the situation isn't perfect here either . . .

My impression of Indian-English poetry? Well, I think it's less well known in the West. I myself don't know enough and I am still learning and absorbing. On the other hand, Indian-English fiction is internationally celebrated. Some of the finest writings in English today are coming out of India. One need only mention, you know, Vikram Seth, Salman Rushdie, Amitav Ghosh and Rohinton Mistry, as well as an older tradition ranging from R.K. Narayan, Raja Rao and Anita Desai. Plainly, this is a very considerable achievement, very substantial body that the British would look at with envy.

SM: Who do you think are the most influential members of the Irish poets writing in English today?

BM: Of the Irish poets, well, obviously Seamus Heaney. And I think that would have been true even before the Nobel Prize. But alongside him, you got somebody like Paul Muldoon who is younger, now living and working in the U.S. You have Tom Paulin, Northern Irish poet. You have Derek Mahon and Michael Longl who are also in our anthology. You have younger poets who have come through since our anthologies: Paul Duroan who deserves attention too. So there's a good number.

SM: How would you contrast the achievement of a poet like Seamus Heaney with that of, say, W.B. Yeats?

BM: Well, you know, looking at Yeats' development is to look at the impact of Modernism upon him, in the way he revised his work and the way in which Ezra Pound and Modernism simply changed the poet he was and made him a modern poet. Seamus Heaney, coming along later, much later, has a very different sort of stance and a very different position vis-à-vis Modernism. He is so assimilated that he can afford to be almost old-fashioned. His verse forms are rather formal, I think. Some critics, including A. Alvarez, have seen him as rather old-fashioned. I don't myself.

A Wandering Writer Finds Home

In this interview, I talk with Farrukh Dhondy about his early life, his stormy encounters with Arundhati Roy, and his views on the current state of Indian culture.

Playwright, novelist, short story writer, critic and media personality, Farrukh Dhondy was born in Poona in 1944. He read Natural Sciences and English at Cambridge University, then took an MA at Leicester before teaching in London for a decade. His published works include *East End at Your Feet, The Siege of Babylon, Come to Mecca, Poona Company* and *Bombay Duck*. He has also written plays for the stage, some of which have been on BBC Television and Channel 4. As a commissioning editor, Dhondy's assignments included outstanding Indian feature films like *Salaam Bombay, Bandit Queen, Electric Moon, Immaculate Conception* and *Mississippi Masala*.

After thirteen years with Channel 4, Dhondy has bowed out. He co-ordinated finally *Indian Summer*, marking the fiftieth anniversary of Indian Independence, the Partition of the subcontinent and the creation of Pakistan.

In this freewheeling interview with me, Farrukh Dhondy, iconoclast and multicultural novelist, looks back at his early life of struggle, his political activism, and profession as a teacher in the UK and his stint as a practical playwright seeking to transform the British society.

Dhondy, who was in India for a British Council seminar, was in his room at the Taj Mahal Hotel, Lucknow, overlooking the poolside banquet in progress. He had already spoken to half-a-dozen journalists. But his mind continued to be razor-sharp and his expression full of wit and humour even though he appeared somewhat tired.

Excerpts from the Interview

SM: How and when did you decide to emigrate to England?

FD: I wanted to study abroad. I spent the last year for my BSc in India and I thought to myself: "I have got to get out of this country! Otherwise I will end up being a research physicist or a research chemist, or some kind of an engineering apprentice." I wanted to get out! I wanted to see the world! I wanted to enlarge my life and not be someone who goes from BSc to MSc to seek employment. I got a Tata scholarship and got admission at Cambridge University. It was the biggest thing that happened in my life.

SM: Did you think that you would stay on? Settle down and make a living in UK?

FD: I was of course in Cambridge for three years. My Indian girlfriend had come with me to England. And after I finished at Cambridge and got my degree, they said, "We need your room for the next person, so please go!" There was nowhere to go! I went to London where my future wife and I shared a room in a basement. I had no money. All the other students from my university, my contemporary Indians, returned, came back home. There were two, three factors—one was, I had no money to travel. I had no cash! Two, I had no means of getting hold of any. And three, my parents at that time were not in India. There was no family home to which to return. My parents had gone to Iran. You might say, immigrant labour; my father was an engineer. So, home would have been to go to Iran. To do what? Going back to my aunt in Poona was also home. To do what? I had no family or influential connections to get a job. So, money, love, politics kept me in Britain!

SM: What was your experience in editing *Ranters, Ravers and Rhymes: Poems by Black and Asian Poets* (1991, Collins)?

FD: Rosemary Stones of Collins asked me to put this anthology together and it was supposed to be for a particular age range. Very particular! And she said, "Use your judgement. You have been a school teacher; see which poems you like." That's what it's all about. This anthology for 16-17 year olds! I had to choose, and the first fundamental choice I made was to think: "Let's take the Black British writers first, which means the Asians as well as the West Indies, Kenyan and African, then go to Africa to West Indies to India. We leave out Black American poets and Black American lyrics, because that's a huge book on its own. We leave out Indian writing translated in English because they won't directly bite into the consciousness of my target audience in Britain. So, that was the job. I had thousands of poems to get through and I suppose I did it!

SM: Every editor has a tough task of inclusion and exclusion. How did you go about it?

FD: It was my anthology, you know! What would I do myself, that was the first criterion. What would I listen to or read? I read through the poems; I went through the poems looking at that. First of all, I chose from memory. So, fifty percent of the book is all that I chose from memory. I remember this poem of Gieve Patel that I loved. There was also a Nissim Ezekiel's poem, as well as one by Dom Moraes that I really liked. And I remembered to look for them, found them, and put them together. For the rest, I had to go through anthologies and original materials. It was me liking it, and I realise that it would connect to teenage readers.

SM: How was the anthology received in Britain?

FD: It was quite well received. It didn't make a great sensation, it made no huge splash on the pond! But that didn't matter.

SM: Would you like to tell us a little more about your life in Britain during this period?

FD: Well, I became a schoolteacher for my living. Not because I had a great vocation to be a schoolteacher, but it seemed a right kind of profession to get into while I wanted to write.

SM: And what did you do in Cambridge?

FD: I didn't do a PhD. I did an undergraduate course. I did a Physics degree. After Part II, I immediately switched to English . . . I took up teaching because I wanted to earn some money.

SM: And when was this?

FD: Between 1969-70. I tried teaching for a while. Then I got admitted into Leicester University to study Modern English and American Literature. I did a thesis on Rudyard Kipling and I read a lot of Modern literature. Two years later, I lived in Leicester in the immigrant district because that was the only place where I could get a room. We lived in a room under the stairs. It was actually one room divided into two, and it had a bathroom outside. It was a nice sweet little flat—alright for a graduate student and his girlfriend. Mala also didn't have much money. And we used to go to a pub round the corner once a week to have a half-pint of beer. Every time I went to the pub, there were groups of Indian workers and they noticed us. They were all industrial workers. We used to meet them regularly and greet them with our politics and what not! We were at that time Communist-Marxists. We were recruited straight into the Indian Workers Association!

SM: And what do you remember as the most significant achievements during this phase?

FD: I became a Secretary of the Indian Workers' Association; not the official one, though. We went to Birmingham and then to London. After a spell in teaching, I joined the Black Panther's Movement because there was no Indian Workers Association where I lived.

SM: The Black Panther Movement with its radical ideology, is it the same that had its origin in America?

FD: Yes, radical. Except, you know, in America it had an armed resistance programme. In Britain, it was a movement of protest. It excited a lot of people to organise themselves very well. It was much like an Indian political party.

SM: Because of such activities, you think you became a kind of persona-non-grata by the authority or the State in Britain?

FD: No. England tolerates dissent. It tolerates radicals! It keeps an eye on them! It keeps a police record on you! So, MI6 might have a whole file on you. As for me, I hit a policeman, was arrested, did some agitation here and there. But as a schoolteacher, I began to write. In magazines, I used to write school articles and stories about what was going on in my classrooms, playground. You know, fiction based on facts.

SM: How did you get interested in the Socialist Movement in the first place? Your interest in the working class?

FD: I believe that every middle class child in India is subject to two or three elementary pressures. One is that they see, at least in my case, a lot of things that we didn't understand. I saw poverty, and you always ask your parents, why are these people not eating? Why are they doing this? You know, everybody asked that because we didn't live in the countryside. We lived in the city. And we seek that all the time. Then, you know, there are disparities and class. For instance, the *ayah* that brought you up! Why is she poor? And then in my teens, I began to understand that the world was divided into rational things and irrational things. I began to understand and appreciate the rational—Mathematics, Physics, books—and then I began to wonder what is religion doing around our necks? What was all these *Jhing Jhing* . . . Hinduism and Islam! Zoroastrian etc. muttering prayers that you don't understand! Languages you don't comprehend! Buga, buga rituals, superstitions! Everyone believes in such words; we had habits of minds, you know! As a young man, I rebelled violently against irrationality. These are the impulses that move you, propel you to ask questions. Poverty, social inequality, superstition and mumbo-jumbo! I believe every middle class child has this.

SM: *East End at Your Feet* heralded the arrival of a new major writer for teenagers. Now, what prompted you to write about the experience of the "inner city" kids?

FD: You can imagine that with my socialistic background, I had two preoccupations. Come Monday morning, Tuesday morning, you have to do a programme for the ordinary people, get them to respond. You are watching them all the time and they become friends. I was immersed in their resistance. Two, I felt that literary London didn't exist for me as I didn't want to be a part of it. I wanted to write a book. I didn't want the book to be reviewed and get myself into some club or things like that. I wanted an audience on whom the book might have an effect. I wanted a larger audience!

SM: In England, you are known as a multicultural writer. Do you feel comfortable by such a description? Do you think that is an attempt to put you in any slot?

FD: I don't mind slotting, I don't mind non-slotting. I don't mind people trying to categorise. By and large, quarrels over categories are either by people who are very careful or by idle minds!

SM: How did you gravitate from literature to cinema? More particularly, as the commissioning editor for Channel 4?

FD: It's quite simple and logical. I wrote short stories. A guy asked me to write stage plays in the early eighties. After I wrote those plays, I was invited to the television. Then I wrote a whole series of stories for television. That was money! Real money! Someone in Channel 4 asked me, "You are a good writer, will you spare a few years and be our commissioning editor?"

SM: And looking back, what do you think have been some of your more significant achievements with Channel 4?

FD: Well, I think of *Salaam Bombay, Mississippi Masala, Train to Pakistan, Kama Sutra, Electric Moon, Immaculate Con-*

ception and *Bandit Queen*. You see, the overall theory I had in Channel 4—twelve years of my life—and what I did in that time was that I brought multiculturalism into the mainstream of British television. Before that, it was not there.

SM: How did you handle the controversies?

FD: You remember the biggest controversy was, of course, over *Bandit Queen*.

SM: The controversy over the debate involving Arundhati Roy and Shekhar Kapoor?

FD: Yes. Arundhati Roy, before she became notorious for getting large cheques, for no reason I can fathom, saw the preview of the film with Bobby Bedi as the producer and said that she would go to court and stop the film from being screened. And Phoolan Devi and her husband thought, fine, they could make money out of it! A French company wanted to sue the film because they themselves wanted to make some money. Robert Lafont, of that company, financed Phoolan Devi. Arundhati picked on that and went through the small gang of two or three people. She took this film to court to stop it being shown internationally. She did the film, at the end, a lot of good because the attention that it got was tremendous. But one nasty thing she did was to stop Shekhar Kapoor from applying to the American Academy. They said the Indian court had instructed them to withdraw the nomination!

SM: You think that Shekhar Kapoor would have won the Oscar?

FD: Oh, he would have won the Oscar! There was no competition that year for the international Oscar. And she went to a judge and had it pulled out. Now, that has not done Shekhar any harm, you know. Shekhar has probably earned some money in the bargain. But it's mean! It's completely purposeless! Because in the end, Phoolan Devi took Channel 4 money. She told Arundhati Roy to go to hell.

SM: Tell me, I'm just being curious. How much money did Channel 4 pay Phoolan Devi?

FD: We gave £40,000! And the distributors gave her husband another £40,000.

SM: And you had no dealings with Arundhati Roy?

FD: I was with Channel 4, and it had to pay to fight the court case, during the course of which Arundhati Roy started getting her friends to write to Channel 4 to throw me out of a job. For making *Bandit Queen*!

SM: So, your experience with Arundhati Roy has not been favourable!

FD: It's totally negative. And totally inexplicable! Unless, she really was working for the French company. I don't understand it.

SM: Why are you now bowing out of Channel 4 after thirteen years of experience with the fascinating medium of cinema?

FD: Because I want to write and want to get some money for writing. As a Channel 4 official, I couldn't get any money for writing. And I didn't have enough time to write films, novels.

SM: If you were to look back at the achievements of Indian-English writing in the last fifty years, which landmarks would you pick up?

FD: I think there have been significant movements. There has been interesting writing. But I don't think, by and large, that Indian fiction has looked at life, phenomenon and society in new ways of seeing. This latest wave of novels has been terribly imitative. People say they are like Laurence Sterne, they are like Gunther Grass, or somebody has picked up a little of James Joyce. It doesn't make for terribly original form! I think V.S. Naipaul has looked at India in a very fresh way. But from the outside! There were several movements in Indian Literature. There were the progressives. Of the thirties and forties, if you like! It's one way to write about thirty years of literature!

"The Deconstructionist Era is Over"

Malcolm Bradbury distinguished British novelist, literary journalist, and cultural ambassador, talks about his fiction, the place of the writer during the post-War years, and the future of literary theory.

I met Malcolm Bradbury at Cambridge. Suave, affable and articulate, Professor Bradbury has been a professor of American Studies at the University of East Anglia since 1970. Currently, he is professor Emeritus.

Malcolm Bradbury has had a number of bestselling novels to his credit, and many critical works including *The Modern British Novel* (1993). He has written for the television and has been an eminent literary journalist.

Excerpts from the Interview

SM: How did you begin writing fiction in the first place?

MB: Well, I started writing in 1952. I suppose that was the only thing I knew at that time. Nottingham was not a very exciting place then!

SM: What was your class background?

MB: My father was a railway man, working class, upper working class. Certainly not from the academic background.

SM: Did you encounter a lot of difficulties in your desire to join the academic profession?

MB: You know, after 1945, there was a new attitude to education. There were free grants to go to the universities. It didn't cost my parents money. My father felt that I should get a job at the age of fifteen or sixteen. My teachers talked to him and told him that I should stay on till eighteen or so, and try to go to the University. I did so! It was a tiny college next to the University of London. I wrote a novel about it.

SM: Is it called *Eating People is Wrong*? What is this novel about?

MB: It is about a red brick university and about a liberal-minded professor who likes to help everybody. He does not quite succeed. It is about liberalism and a kind of academic naiveté. What I was trying to capture was the new social class coming to the university. It is also about the atmosphere of the period after Nazism. My central character had been a Marxist when he was a student. He then gave up Marxism. This was very typical of the period. So I suppose there were two key things—one was campus as a place of social change, and the other was teaching ideological and cultural values. My first book was essentially a comedy. My second one has a setting in an American university (I went to America as a graduate student) and it is about McArthurism and the whole business of interference with teaching by Right-wing figures.

SM: Given the orthodox anti-Communism at that time in America, did you encounter any difficulties on account of your novel?

MB: Not much! I suppose that was partly because the novel was first published in England, and due to various versions, the publication got delayed until after the end of the MacArthurism.

SM: And so it had a good reception?

MB: Yes, a very good reception! My third academic novel is set in a British new University, the kind where I was teaching at that time. It is about the student radicalism of the sixties and a teacher who wants to capitalise on this for his interest. It was a kind of seventies response to the sixties. The campus novel was getting caught with events, the changing political life, the changing cultural life, and then after that, the campus no longer seemed to be a stage for such interesting stories. I realised I could go on writing comedies of academic life which would be kind of repetitious. And so I wrote novels dealing with the experience in Eastern Europe.

SM: What novels of this category did you write?

MB: The chief one is *Rates of Exchange*. It is about Eastern Europe during the time of the Cold War, and another one, *Dr. Criminalis*, is about the period after the Cold War, 1989. The novel that I'm writing now is a kind of summing up, in a way, of the theme that I have been dealing with, namely philosophy, politics, high society, corruption, and the satirical responses you can have to all these things.

SM: I understand that is forthcoming soon. Now, many readers have found international experience in your writings. Many of your novels can be described as international novels. How much of the Indian experience, if at all, has been reflected in any of your novels, and to what extent has your personality as a writer been influenced by the Indian experience?

MB: There are various answers to that. One is that E.M. Forster has influenced me. I knew Forster at Cambridge and wrote a couple of books about him, and because of that I had a lot of Indian graduate students who are also working on Forster, including people with whom I stayed in touch with like U.R. Ananthamurthy, Raja Rao, etc. I also came to know a lot of Indian writers who are based in England and in America—Vikram Chandra, Arundhati Roy, Salman Rushdie, and so on.

SM: Have you ever been to India?

MB: No, I have never been. I was about to come three years ago. Unfortunately, I fell ill and I could not come!

SM: You belong to a generation where people swore in terms of classics as against journalism and popular literature. It goes to your credit that you never believed in those kinds of watertight compartments. Today, of course, popular literature is accepted as part of the academia. How did it feel to have such views in those days?

MB: The crucial thing, of course, was that I was first and foremost a writer and less of a professor. I did television when it was first introduced in Britain. I was also involved in films. I started creative writing courses in a university in England . . .

SM: Was it in East Anglia?

MB: Yes, exactly!

SM: What major events in filmmaking do you remember? Was it in script writing?

MB: I have written for an enormous number on TV.

SM: You also carried out literary journalism. For which leading newspapers did you write?

MB: Almost all of them! *The TLS, The Times London, The New Statesman, The Guardian,* and the American ones as well. *New York Times, Boston Globe, The New Yorker, Washington Post*, papers all over the world!

SM: In many parts of the world, you have been perceived as an icon of the best part of British culture and literature. How did it feel to be so? It must have been certainly a very heady experience for you to be sought after so much in so many different parts of the world as a cultural ambassador. What was the experience like?

MB: Well, as I said, these were very interesting moments! I was part of the first literary group sent by the British Government to China after the Cultural Revolution. I've enjoyed the experience. I have been very fortunate both as an academic and as a writer.

SM: Your criticism and theory have been very well received. Did you ever find any contradiction in pursuing both? Many creative writers feel that criticism kills their creativity. What is your view?

MB: Modern literary criticism and theory seem to diverge from creative practice. It seems almost impossible to keep up with both. I had a way out. If I did not like theory such as deconstruction, I could always teach creative writing.

SM: Many of the post-structuralist theorists seem to be giving a secondary status to creative writing. At one level, such a state appears to be absurd because criticism is also supposed to serve the interest of literature and not to supplant it. Do you feel disturbed by this?

MB: Yes, to a point that was true for twenty to twenty-five years. I think it's reverse now. I think the post-structuralist or the deconstructionist era is over really. Now the problem is the opposite, anything goes!

SM: Cultural relativism?

MB: Exactly, and the problem of having critical standards. The critic becomes more desirable when you want to make judgements, and so I am more sympathetic to criticism than I was a few years ago.

SM: You have had many influential positions such as in the Cambridge Seminar, and I'm sure you have been the chairperson of many juries for judging outstanding literature. Can you recall any special literary event when you were able to give a sense of direction?

MB: You know that I was the Chairman of the judges for the Booker Prize when *Midnight's Children* was an unknown book and Rushdie was an unknown author until he won that prize. I gave him a fortunate or unfortunate life as a result of this! It was also an interesting moment in the life of the Booker because most of the writers before that were fairly well known and had been rewarded because of their fame, while an unknown writer won this time. In a sense, there was a hunger for a new generation of writing in Britain at that time, and so the prize reflected a search for that kind of writer, and that was a key moment!

SM: May I say you look remarkably fit? I am curious to know how old you are!

MB: I am sixty-six!

SM: You certainly don't look it. How do you keep yourself fit, do you go for a jog?

MB: I mostly write, actually (laughs). I am still an Emeritus professor, you know!

Out of the Shadows

Namita Gokhale, eminent novelist and short story writer, talks about her debut novel Paro, *her views on the art of fiction, and her latest publication* The Book of Shadows, *Penguin India.*

Excerpts from the Interview

SM: What is *The Book of Shadows* all about?

NG: It is a book that had me quite puzzled! It is a ghost story. It is also an esoteric novel at some level. It has a sandwich kind of a structure with three layers of consciousness. The primary story at one level is told by a young girl called Rachita who is a lecturer in English in a college in Delhi. She has acid thrown on her face by her lover, and she has some blurring of the reality. She is having a bad time. She goes to the old house in the hills to recover. There she encounters some old stories of the house, which enter her consciousness and make her the vehicle of articulating that story. This is actually the framework for the real story, a story of the ghost who lives in that house and is examining the lives of the humans who live there. It is a colonial house, a house built sometime in the early part of the nineteenth century by a missionary. And there are books of that missionary where we really see the missionary point of view of colonising the experience, the missionary's reaction to the new landscape.

SM: So the story is set in the hills of UP?

NG: Yes.

SM: And the time?

NG: Late last century, early this century. A bit of the present as well. It is very important to me to have a specificity of the locale. I love the hills very much, and we are very animistic about our hills. We have our little place gods, and we believe there are power spots too. And so, this book is about this particular spot, the house.

SM: Are there Indian characters as well as English men? Can we therefore describe it largely as an Indo-British cultural encounter?

NG: (Shakes her head) No!

SM: It's different from that?

NG: It's an encounter between dimensions. And it's really about the frontier of the consciousness, it's an old-fashioned ghost story!

SM: We'll come back to the details of the narrative, but tell me, is it a continuation of your earliest book *Paro* in some sense, or does it make a complete break from *Paro*?

NG: No, I think the voice of the college lecturer is very much like the voice of Paro, the voice of the urban Indian woman. But whereas *Paro* dealt with the contradictions of Delhi and Bombay's social life and the slightly bizarre sensibility of an upper middle class Indian life, this book travels in a somewhat different direction.

SM: I'm curious to know the circumstances in your life that preceded your life as a writer.

NG: I am from Nainital, and this has always been an important part of my being. People may be lost in their new cosmopolitan wilderness, but I have a primary identity as a Kumaoni Brahmin girl. Even the "brahmin" part is important, not in terms of caste but in terms of the way one thinks, the attitude one has. I am very close to the soil of that place. My last three books have been in the soil of the hills.

SM: At what point in time did you start writing creatively?

NG: Well, I never wrote much poetry. I was really bad at poetry, but I wrote short stories at the college level . . . I was really thrown out of the college!

SM: I didn't know that! How on earth did it happen? Tell me in brief.

NG: It can't be brief! I was in Jesus and Mary College, which is immortalised in my book. This is what the writers do. We take our little revenges! So, I was chucked out of college, JMC, in 1973-74. And I have taken revenge against a character who teaches in JMC. To cut a long story short, a nun was upset with me because I chose to read a course in Hindi literature which included authors like Mohan Rakesh rather than a course on Chaucer. As a result, I went to court, and in a limited way I won the case. But since it was a minority college, they had their way. And thus, I'm not a graduate!

SM: Around this time you got married?

NG: No, I was already married. I was already in publishing. My husband and I met over a magazine called *Embryo*, and the natural joke was the embryo got aborted! We got Shiva Naipaul to give us an original short story and we got an interview with Margaret Mead, the anthropologist. We also got a very intelligent lecturer called Meenakshi Mukherjee, who was not so well known then as she is now, to write an article for us called "Who is Afraid of Enid Blyton," which was later published in *Times of India*! Then I started a film magazine.

SM: I was coming to that. How did it happen?

NG: I was the publisher. The editor was someone called Rauf Ahmed, very bright, who was with *Filmfare* after that.

SM: Was it like "Stardust?"

NG: A little brighter than that!

SM: How long did it last?

NG: Eight years. It was quite respectable in Bombay. The turning point in my career as a novelist came when I saw an Englishman taking notes to write a novel. I thought I could also take notes and write one myself, and some of the basic rules for writing a novel came to me. The basic rule is, "just carry on!" That is the mantra of writing a novel!

SM: You mean without a central design or anything?

NG: You have got to have the courage to go on and on! You can't wait for the perfect beginning or the perfect ending, and somehow it all comes together at the end. That's what works for me! When I started writing this novel . .

SM: When was it?

NG: Somewhere around 1983. You know, daily life in India is so strange and bizarre! The lives of the rich are so disconnected and so ironic, and *Paro* was really a spoof on the gothic novel! I have always been fond of "low" art and "low" literature. I read my share of romantic novels. I was looking at the Gothic literature and the romantic novels, the wish-fulfilment of the dull and mousy girl who gets the rich husband. In actual life, of course, it is not the dull and mousy girl who gets the rich husband!

SM: Have you read Shobha De's *Starry Nights*? She seems to be using the same style.

NG: Shobha De, I'm sorry to say, really picked up the style after my novel was published!

SM: This is what you claim?

NG: I'm not claiming, I'm stating facts! She has picked up not my style, but the genre of the "Saree Ripper!" But I did it in an ironic framework, whereas she did it in a more straight commercial manner. *Paro* was the grandmother of all these novels! And as far as the reception in India, I was treated in some quarters as a writer of pornographical novels, especially because I came from a respectable family. My father was a politician. I wore a saree and I looked like I was betraying the class I belonged to. I was given a very hard time. There was a huge degree of sensationalist reaction rather than a literary one, which led me into a long silence. I really thought that I'm not a literary writer. Of course, by now I have written five books. *Gods, Graves and Grandmother* got very good reviews in India. Slowly, people were beginning to take me as a writer and not as a sexual oddity!

SM: Who are your literary ideals?

NG: The only author I really admire is Muriel Spark.

SM: You don't think much of Indian-English female writers like Nayantara Sahgal and Kamala Markandeya?

NG: Well, I don't dislike them! In fact, Nayantara Sahgal is a wonderful writer. But she is not presenting life on the edge, which my novels do. I don't relate to her world! All the same, I think she is a wonderful writer. So is Anita Desai. And as for me, *The Book of Shadows*, let me say with a straight face that the book has a lot of "automatic" writing in it. You know, there is a world of psychic phenomena beyond our doors of perception. One can also enter into that twilight zone! I believe that with the circumstances of my life, my husband's tragic demise, and my illness, I was particularly prone to that world! I was not conscious as a writer as to which part of my subconsciousness was working. I have also had a lot of religious experience. I mean, if you are an Indian, in some ways, religion is bound to be central to your understanding.

SM: What do you do for a living?

NG: I write, you know (laughs). As my sister says, I am like the old mothers in the Hindi films who have to constantly do things like stitching clothes for a livelihood! I write for anybody who asks me to write on any subject, whether or not I am competent to write about it. And I'm also a consultant to various development projects.

SM: What is your next plan? Next writing project?

NG: I have already begun two books. I don't know which one will gather momentum first.

Translation as a Form of Negotiation

Susan Bassnett advocated translation studies when it was unfashionable in the academia to do so. Today, she is acknowledged as a pioneer. She spoke to the author on a wide range of issues related to translation studies. Translation, in theory and practice, has today emerged from the periphery to the central stage. How has this happened? Can there be an ethic for a good translator? Susan Bassnett answers these and related questions.

Susan Bassnett is Professor at the Centre for British Translation and Culture Studies at the Warwick University. She is also the pro-Vice Chancellor at the same university. Internationally renowned as a pioneer in the field of translation studies, Professor Bassnett is avidly sought after in the conference circuit. Dr. Bassnett was in Chennai in October 1998 to chair the British Council-*The Hindu* seminar on "The Banyan and the Oak: Translation and Cultural Representation in South India."

Dr. Bassnett's trip to India (the first ever) was somewhat dramatic. Literally chasing Gulf-Air flights at Abu Dhabi and Muscat, she finally prevailed upon Air India to take her to India: "I have to be there at the inauguration of this important seminar," she announced before the somewhat sceptical Air India official at Muscat. From Thiruvanthapuram, she flew in to Chennai. While others would have asked for two days to recover from jet lag and a Middle-Eastern adventure, Professor Bassnett was fresh as a daisy when she spoke to me, a fellow-participant at the same seminar.

Excerpts from the Interview

SM: Translation study is increasingly gaining ground in the academia. But it was not always so. How does it feel to be at the centre from the one-time periphery?

SB: Actually, it feels terribly good to see translation at the centre. I think this has been a pattern with many subjects over the last two decades. You can see this in gender studies, post-colonial studies, and also with translation. When I recall some of my colleagues twenty years ago saying that translation was a waste of time and that the study of translation was pointless, then yes, I can feel quite pleased!

SM: The traditional approach to the subject of translation was guided by what George Steiner calls the fidelity-betrayal syndrome, that a translated text ought to be "faithful" to the so-called "original." What accounts for the persistence of such a view for so long?

SB: This is an interesting question. Through the centuries, there has been a debate as to how faithful a translation ought to be, and faithful to whom, should the translation be faithful to the author or to those who cannot read the original language? I think the reason the view continues is because people who are not translators believe that there ought to be certainties and fixed rules. I think there is a great drive in human nature for certainties, and people want to be told: "This is faithful" and "this isn't it." I think the process is much more complex than that. I think translation is all about negotiating, negotiating the world of the original author and the world of the reader.

SM: Do you think that translation activity forms an integral part of cultural activity everywhere?

SB: I'd say that translation is a fundamental human activity. I often say to my students that even people who don't know any other language, who know only one language, are engaged in translating; they're engaged in some form of translation activity all the time. Of course, they don't speak the same way. For example, when they're speaking to their grandparents, when they're addressing their friends, or when they're addressing their employers, they actually use different kinds of languages; they translate their thoughts. You could go even farther and say that all thought, the moment it's put into words, is effectively a kind of translation. This is what Mexican writer Octavio Paz argues. He says that the actual act of speech is a translation of thought. And so, translation is a very, very fundamental activity.

SM: Translation theories often use terms like "foreignisation" and "domestication"—terms first used by the critic Lawrence Vinuti. In what ways do these terms illuminate our understanding of the subject?

SB: These are indeed very interesting terms that Vinuti talks about. Some people also refer to "domestication" as "acculturation." Such terms bring to attention the fact that there are different translation conventions that operate in different cultures, in different times. Translators ought to try and make tests from other cultures appear like tests written by nature writers. This is part of what one may call the domestication process. At other times, there is a very clear attempt to keep the translated text free from certain translations. For instance, in some European languages, one never translates names. On the other hand, among the nature Americans, in the North American context, the convention has been to domesticate names. I'd say that in both these cases, there are pretty profound ideological implications.

SM: While some consider translation as derivative, others, especially in the field, have argued in recent times that it is more challenging creatively. In what sense does it pose a greater challenge?

SB: I've always found translation enormously challenging. I don't see myself primarily as a theorist. I see myself as someone whose theory is rooted in practice. I've just finished putting together a manuscript that Dangaroo Press is publishing, together with some of my poetry. I've called it a manuscript of poems and translations. It's called *Exchanging Lives* because I wanted to draw attention to the creativity of translation. I think it's a grave mistake to think of translation as some kind of slavish activity where the translator just needs a dictionary and a minimum knowledge of language in reproducing something. Translation, I'd say, is very definitely a re-creation.

SM: Professor Bassnett, sometimes, translation becomes a shaping force for literary change and development. At times, it creates new genres, and shapes the literary sensibility as well. How is it so? Could you give some examples of this process?

SB: This of course to me is one of the most exciting aspects of translation studies over the last twenty years. It has finally been recognised that translation can be a huge powerful force in shaping literature. One of the best examples one can think of is the European example. You can think of a sonnet or a similar form that originates in Italian, and that in the space of two centuries, spreads across the European literatures, changing its nature very slightly as it goes, so that by the time you have the Shakespearean sonnet, it is very different from the Petrarchan sonnet. But you wouldn't have had the Shakespearean sonnet if you didn't have translation. And the corollary to the question is: "Why do some texts not become a shaping force in literary change?" So I think there are lots of fascinating questions here about literary history.

SM: Do you think there ought to be an ethic for a translator? How do you judge the quality of a good translation?

SB: The question of ethic is a very interesting one. It has not been fashionable in North America or Europe to talk about morality and literature. And I think the tide is turning now. I think now the moral and the ethnical questions are coming back on the agenda. If you look at the actual terms of reference of the International Federation of Translators, with reference to instructions to translators, there are ethical questions raised there. One of the points is that if the translator does not agree with the ideology or contents of a text, he or she should not translate it; the translator should not go against his moral principles. I think the question of the morality of the translator is probably something that is going to occupy us over the next few years. I can see this becoming a very big issue.

And linked to that, of course, is the question of quality. This again is a problem because Western literary tradition has for twenty or thirty years not wanted to make value judgements. Of course, we all say, this is a good translation, that is a bad translation. So we must have some criteria. And I think it is important to remember the historical dimension. What was deemed to be a wonderful translation in 1860 might be hopeless in 1920, fashionable in 1950 and dead in 1990. So we need to take this aspect into account.

SM: What were the primary objectives for starting the Warwick seminar on literary translation? (I recall my own participation as a memorable event.) To what extent have these objectives been fulfilled?

SB: The Warwick seminars were quite simply seminars that we built out of our own teaching. Our approach in Warwick has been to combine translation along with culture. This explains my own interest in translation and travel writing. I think translation needs to be seen in the cultural context, whereas some scholars and some universities have favoured a linguistic approach. The Warwick approach has been cultural. I think our seminars have been quite successful and a lot of talented colleagues from many parts of the world have taken part in the seminar. We can also see this in the very large number of PhD students we now have from different parts of the world working on issues on translation and culture.

SM: Culture theory today favours diversity and multiculturalism, and yet the official sponsors of translation seem to rely on the need for unity of some sort, say, pan Indian or pan

European. How can we reconcile these differences in approach? Should we take a closer look at the State funding of translation activity?

SB: This question no doubt refers to the political aspects of translation. I think you're absolutely right in that translation is a highly political activity. I entirely agree with you that we should look at the whole question of State funding of translation. I think we should also look at those states that don't fund translation. When you think of English-speaking states such as the United Kingdom or the United States, you find that the funding for translation there is absolutely abysmal. Of course, it is much better in Canada, but Canada in any case is a bilingual State.

SM: In India, especially during the colonial period, we have encountered what can be defined as the missionary model of translation, where a lot of distortions took place on cultural and ideological grounds. There has been a conscious attempt to get out of this model in post-Independent India. Do you think that a secular Western model has now replaced the earlier one? Do you think that Western science and knowledge systems have taken the place of the missionary model of translation?

SB: Well, I think the notion of the missionary model sounds fairly absurd. I think though that it would be a grave mistake for a country like India with so many languages, so many diverse literary traditions, so many models to choose from, to opt for imported models. I think in the whole field of translation, what we are involved in is a discussion on greater diversity. The discussion involves change, it involves looking at a range of different models. We need to look at our own traditions as well.

SM: A hierarchy of languages and cultures seems to prevail when it comes to translating texts from non-Western languages into English. Clearly, there seems to be a resistance in the Western academia, and publishers in the West are reluctant to take up such projects. How can such imbalances be rectified?

SB: This is really a very tough question. Western publishers are increasingly aiming at the market. It's a constant problem not only for what I'd call non-Western literatures but also non-mainstream Western literature. The writers from Poland or Sweden or Portugal face the same problem. It's a question, I suppose, of two things really. One is to try and feed into the system, you know, doing one's best, really, to try and bring to attention the publications in the Macmillan and Heinemann series. The other way would be to work with small publishers. I keep advising people, for instance, that instead of trying to sell a whole book of short stories to a publisher, maybe it would be a good idea to sell one story to a magazine like *Granta* or *The New York Review of Books*. That creates a market because publishing is very, very market-driven. The other possibility is a collaboration, and that seems to be a way out. I think these could be some of the strategies.

SM: How is translation playing a role in the creation of the European Union?

SB: It's a very good question. What the European Union has done is to put translation really on the map. There is always a problem of minority and majority languages. All the same, what you've now got is a lot of countries in the European Union that have come into prominence in the field of translation and interpretation. Take, for instance, Finland and the Czech Republic. Previously, their languages were virtually unknown. The European Union has also done a lot to help minority languages.

SM: Though you're an acknowledged authority in the field, there are bound to be some areas in the domain of translation that must have baffled and intrigued you. What are these?

SB: I suppose we are all baffled by the aspect of the untranslatable because it is entirely culture-bound. What do you exactly do? I am inclined to take a kind of middle view. I think it's very important to trust the readers' intelligence. Readers are intelligent; they will always try and work it out. But I also think that there are times when without footnotes, the whole thing collapses. So I think this is the hardest part.

SM: Would you tell us something about the state of the art of translation in England and in the continent? I know you've already given broad indications.

SB: Well, the state of translation in Britain is, frankly, terrible. According to Lawrence Vinuti's figure, two-and-a-half percent of the market pertains to translation, and three-and-a-half percent in the U.S. That is only slightly better compared to 65% in Italy and over 70% in Sweden. And so, I think there is really no comparison. Most of Europe translates. In Britain, there is frankly a sense of isolation.

SM: How did you turn to translation in the first place? What languages do you handle as a practising translator?

SB: Well, it's a question that relates to my childhood. You know, as a very young girl I was taken to Denmark. When I learned English, I also learned Danish. Bilingualism, I suppose, is a part of my growing up. I was in different countries. When you are bilingual, you also become bicultural. It also means that you have more perspectives. You see, it gives you a sort of double vision. I don't know whether everybody does this. But when I dream, I dream with a double vision. I wonder if it is connected to duality. I think you can learn something in one language that you cannot in another. You almost go through a kind of personality shift. I have handled languages like French, Spanish and Italian for the purpose of translation.

SM: What are your current projects?

SB: It's hard to define. It's a sort of memoir-cum-travel book. It's a book based on Fielding's journal of his voyage to Lisbon. You know, Fielding travelled to Lisbon and died there. Lisbon is where I spent five years of my childhood between five and ten.

SM: As the daughter of a diplomat?

SB: Yes, and I discovered that I used to play hide and seek when I was a small child around the tomb of Fielding, so I tried to write a sort of return to Lisbon, thinking of its significance. It probably sounds very pretentious. But I have tried to make it acceptable. Let's see how I can get on when I get back.

SM: What about your newspaper articles?

SB: Well, these articles I started when I became the pro-Vice Chancellor. I had less time for pure research. I got very angry with a lot of things like bureaucracy. I thought one way to deal with my anger was to write satirical pieces in papers like *The Independent*. Well, I got a terrific reaction!

SM: A sort of David Lodge?

SB: Sort of! For instance, one of my pieces was on the spuriousness of the quality industry and another was on language, how English was actually being transformed by bureaucrats. I am doing one every three or four weeks, a regular column. I get lots and lots of letters from people saying, "Yes, I've been thinking that for ages!"

SM: What's your final assessment of the Chennai seminar? [This was after the seminar].

SB: Well, I think the seminar—"Translation and Cultural Representation in South India"—was tremendously exciting. I can say honestly that I have seen the part of the best and most animated discussion that I have heard in years. I think clearly that there are all sorts of interesting things happening, in particular in South India. As a purely ignorant Westerner, who unfortunately does not know any of your wonderful languages, I think there is an infinite number of possibilities for translation here. That is why I believe that India has truly become one of the world's centres in the theory and practice of translation. You've got it all here.

"We Don't Sell Art in Our Culture"

Prafulla Mohanti, London-based architect, author and artist, speaks about his experience as a painter and the future of art in the cross-cultural context.

Prafulla Mohanti was born and brought up in the village of Nanpur in Orissa. He went to England after graduating as an architect in Bombay. In 1964, he gained a diploma in town planning at Leeds University, where in the same year his first one-man exhibition of paintings was held. He worked as an architect-planner for the Greater London Council, but now devotes himself to painting and writing. He has taught painting and dancing to children in the East End of London and has given dance recitals relating movement to painting.

He is the author of *My Village, My Life, Indian Village Tales, Through Brown Eyes*, and his latest *Changing Village Changing Life*.

Prafulla Mohanti has held exhibitions in many parts of the world including Europe, America, Japan and India. His paintings have been represented in several international travelling exhibitions.

I met Prafulla Mohanti at his spacious flat on 20 Sussex Street in London. In fact, I spent two days with him and his friend, Derrick. "Come and spend some time with me," he had insisted when I had called him up from Nottingham. On the second day, we returned home after getting our grocery. On the way back, Mr. Mohanti stopped and eyed two big circular tabletops that were dumped thoughtlessly in the neighbourhood garbage bin. He began rolling them towards his flat. "These will be handy for my paintings," he declared, as he began to unscrew the rusted nails and old rexine covers. I lent him a helping hand. Later, we went inside his studio, on the ground floor of his flat. This was the first time I had a look at his place—a collection of various ethnic vases, decorated pots, and Oriya appliqué designs from Pipli competed for space with his paintings, described by some critics as Tantric art—bright concentric circles in red, yellow, aquamarine blue. These constituted the bulk of the display, his signature tune on canvas. "Look, I have put on a bright shirt for you," Mohanti said as he posed for photographs! He spoke of his early upbringing in the village, initiation into the world of village art, and his passionate faith in the need to rescue art from the morass of commercial culture.

Excerpts from the Conversation

SM: You have been a writer, painter, architect and town planner. You have excelled in many fields at the same time. How do you look at yourself as a painter, and how far back can you look?

PM: When I was about three, I was introduced to the village Chatshali by my grandmother, who could not read or write but was determined that her grandson should study. The teacher took my right hand and with a piece of chalk drew three figures—Brahma, Vishnu and Maheswara. Now, I don't know of any other culture where at the age of three you learn to draw three perfect circles, the circles representing divine energy. Looking back, I think it must have induced in the child in me a sense of meditation. When the child opens his eyes and sees his aunt, the village, the environment, the flowers, the people and the various manifestations of Nature, he sees the presence of divine energy everywhere. This then helps him to understand the meaning of relationship with Nature. My drawing and my painting started from then. In the village, we painted the faces, the hands, the flowers for various religious functions. We painted the village deity, the Mahalia Buddha, the Shiva Linga covered with vermilion paste, and I used to watch the attendant painting the deity. I found the red colour very attractive from my childhood. And so I have been painting from the age of three or four.

SM: In your memoir, you have said that your first stay at Leeds and in England produced an acute sense of alienation, that you could not relate to the environment. Consequently, you started filling up your room with very bright Indian art forms. How did this happen? Could you tell me something more about this experience?

PM: You know, when I came to England, I missed my parents, missed my friends, and the colours of India. I was in Leeds, an industrial city. I felt a little more isolated because everything was grey. The room I rented was a Victorian building; the inside was so grey that I just could not relate myself to that grey room and that grey city around me. I could not, of course, buy my culture; you know, I could not go to a shop and buy Indian culture. And so I had to create it. What I did was to cut large pieces of paper and draw the village symbols of Jagannath, the lotus, etc. and put them on the walls of the room. Immediately, the character of the room changed. That helped me to understand that I could create my own environment. That is where my paintings actually started in a very serious way. I would go to the college to attend my classes; and in the evening when I came back, I would paint and draw. The village symbols became personal symbols. It was indeed a process of self-discovery. I enjoyed doing colours and diagrams very much . . .

SM: It seems that the first major breakthrough in your career as a painter came when you were encouraged to put up a one-man exhibition at Leeds University. However, as in the case of other artists, you must have had your share of disappointments as well. How did you handle this phase?

PM: You know, I did not come from a culture where you painted for money. In the village, we painted the walls and that was all for the service of the divine energy. Because I was good at painting, I was constantly invited by the villagers to paint their walls. That gave me encouragement; their appreciation helped me. Even at Leeds, the whole idea of selling was alien to me. In our culture, we always gave away art objects. Selling was considered degrading or demeaning. At Leeds, my college was part of the College of Art. There, the students and teachers saw my works and liked them. Some of them even wanted to exchange mine with their own . . .

SM: What was your experience with the art galleries?

PM: I came to London with a portfolio of my paintings. I went to the private galleries. Some said they liked my paintings but unfortunately did not show that kind of work. Others said that they were more fully booked for two to three years; they were not taking new artists. Later, I was directed to the curator of the Indian section of the V & A (Victoria and Albert Museum), who was rude, terribly rude. I was thoroughly disappointed and returned to Leeds. On the return trip, in the train, I was drawing on a piece of paper. The man next to me seemed to like it and asked: "How much?" I said, "Well, if you like it, you can have it!" My friends at Leeds encouraged me to put up an exhibition at the University. The University bought some of the paintings, the professors bought some. The event was covered by the local press. Then I was covered by other galleries. The City Art Gallery bought a painting. That's how it all started!

SM: Your paintings have often been described as Tantric. Was it a conscious decision to use this style? Can you tell us something about the significance of Tantric art, especially the way it has been experimented in the contemporary context by Indian artists?

PM: I didn't quite know that my work was Tantric. It happened in a natural way. In my village culture, the basic forms that inspired me were the circle, the lotus, Jagannath, his black eyes, the Shalagram, and the Shivalingam; the colours red, blue and yellow. Until I went to an exhibition in Delhi, I didn't know that my work was Tantric. I showed my work to somebody called Birendra Kumar, who was the Director of Kumar Galleries in Delhi. Birendra Kumar thought that my paintings were "perfect examples of Tantric art." Then I realised that perhaps every aspect of Orissa village life was Tantric. For instance, the Shivalingam, the worship of Mangala, the Mother Goddess, the village deity in a stone, the stone covered with vermilion paste—these are all symbols of Tantric art. Interestingly, neither the villagers nor I knew that these were Tantric art.

SM: Of all the motifs found in your paintings, the circle or the Bindu happens to be a recurrent one. Why is it so?

PM: Well, the red spot on my mother's forehead must have been a striking experience for me in my childhood. My mother's face, the sunset, the sunrise, the moon, the planets—these used to fascinate me a lot. If you are born and brought up in an environment close to Nature, the circle and the Bindu become very important. For me, the Bindu is a symbol of life experience.

SM: We know that art forms are culture-specific. At the same time, your paintings have found universal acceptance. How do you explain this phenomenon?

PM: In my work, the village symbols became personal symbols; these in turn became universal symbols. After all, a circle is a circle. In the West, it is a geometrical shape or form, but in India we have a different significance—a circle becomes a Mangala, it takes up various manifestations, especially the divine forms. The colour red, for instance, symbolises Mangala, the Goddess of Energy. When the personal truth and the universal truth become one, the artist is able to communicate universally. I don't quite know why some people like my work. If you look at it, it will have some significance. On the other hand, if my identity is revealed, it will acquire another significance because viewers have association with India and Indian art. For instance, some think that I am an Indian artist from a village and so ought to be doing miniature paintings, gods and goddesses with twenty arms and ten hands. . . . That sort of thing. They could not understand that the basic truth about art and life are the same all over the world.

SM: You belong to a tradition where writers have also been painters. One thinks, for instance, of William Blake, Dante Gabriel Rossetti, and D.H. Lawrence. You have been a writer, an architect, and a dancer. You have excelled in so many forms. What underlying connection do you find in all these sister disciplines?

PM: Let me tell you of an incident. When I was fourteen, I once told my mother that I wanted to go to Shantiniketan to study art. My mother's habit was not to give a definite reply, but tell a story from the Puranas. She told me about a disciple who went to a Guru and said, "Please teach me how to paint." The teacher replied: "Go and study literature. Then learn music, dance, and other art forms. When you have learnt all important aspects of the art form, then only shall I teach you how to paint." What my mother was trying to tell me was that you don't have to go to an art school to learn; you can learn it in the village itself. In the same manner, you can also learn music, art, dance and literature. That helped me understand man's relationship with the environment, the meaning of structure and form. Dance helped me understand movement in expression. All forms are inter-related. In the West, art forms have been fragmented. As a result, there are some specialised art forms that have no relationship with life. My paintings helped me understand the meaning of colour in writing. My architecture made me understand the meaning of structure in writing. Similarly, my knowledge of town planning created in me a greater awareness about the basic needs of human beings and their relationship with the community, and with the environment. It has enabled me to understand life as whole and not as a fragmented thing. What I cannot express in painting, I express in writing, and vice versa.

SM: What do you think ought to be done to prevent the commercialisation of art?

PM: You see, what has happened is that the artist has become a performer. He/she is also producing a commodity to sell. That commodity has very little relevance to our environment, or to our life. It's like money—your ten thousand rupees have no value unless you can exchange that money to buy something. People must buy paintings because then they can exchange the paintings for something else. The question is not what you like in a painting, but how much you can get out of it. That is totally alien to us, to our culture. In London, for instance, you cannot see an artist; you don't even know how the artist was enriched by his environment.

SM: Have you made any effort to implement art in Orissa?

PM: I have started a small school in my village Nanpur in Orissa. It is an art centre where artists and writers come and meet, discuss ideas and work with the village craftsmen while relating art with their environment. What worries me is that the whole of India is a gigantic slum, a spiritual slum. What has happened to the India of my childhood and dreams, I wonder!

SM: Indeed, you are absolutely right!

PM: The artists are totally marginalised; they are considered redundant to the development process. Well, I do hope something can be done. Perhaps I should spend a longer time in Orissa so that alternate ways of looking at art could be developed.

English Studies and Multiculturalism

Professor Alastair Niven is the Head of Literature, British Council, London. He has written two books on D.H. Lawrence as well as on Mulk Raj Anand and Raja Rao. He has, among other things, edited two anthologies of Commonwealth Writing—Under Another Sky *(poetry) and* Enigmas and Arrivals *(fiction). He has taught at the Universities of Ghana, Leeds and Stirling. In this interview, he speaks to me about the relationship between English Studies and multiculturalism.*

Alastair Niven has had a distinguished career as an educational administrator. He was the Director-General of Africa Centre, London (1978-84), Chapman Fellow at the Institute of Commonwealth Studies, University of London (1984-85), Director of Literature, Arts Council of England (formerly Great Britain) (1987-97). He has had varied international experience in the field of promoting commonwealth and post-colonial literatures. In India, he chaired a three-day national seminar at Lucknow (4-6 February 1988), which brought together leading British and Indian writers, poets and critics. Later, on a visit to the University of Hyderabad, where he and Winsome Pinnock, leading Black woman playwright, addressed the Department of English, Professor Niven spoke to me on his current responsibilities as the Head of Literature, British Council. He also spoke about his vision for expanding commonwealth and post-colonial literature in the field of British literary studies, and British Council Library's plan of forthcoming activities in India; his life as an educational administrator, his love of D.H. Lawrence, and above all, the place he sees for literature in an increasingly technological and consumer society.

Excerpts from the Interview

SM: You have been a scholar of repute in the field of English literature before being an educational administrator. What was the transition like? Was it smooth?

AN: I think the transition has been reasonably smooth, though I must confess missing some aspects of academic life a lot. I would like more time to write, although I do try to write short pieces. I am not so sure I miss the teaching as much as I feel I should do, because frankly, I got quite tired of marking students' essays when so many of them seem to say exactly the same things. I do admire teachers, however. I think at the same time that I would not make a distinction between the world of the academic scholar and the world of the educational administrator because both are concerned with knowledge and culture. In my place, I have been able to facilitate through my role as the Director of Literature in the Arts Council of Great Britain and now as the Director of Literature in British Council.

SM: Much before the writers of the Commonwealth became accepted as part of the literary canon, you had chosen to work on some of the non-White writers of the Commonwealth for your MA as well as your PhD. How did it happen?

AN: Well, it really happened almost by chance. I was in my last years in Cambridge University and I was wondering what to do next. I decided that I wanted to go abroad for a while because I had not travelled outside Europe. I was awarded the Commonwealth scholarship, as a consequence of which I was sent to West Africa. And in Ghana I studied African literature. This was of great interest to me and led me later to all kinds of literature in English written abroad. Perhaps in my family background there was a vigorous encouragement for such an affair because my grandparents spent thirty-five years in India, and my father was brought up in his early life in India. So I suppose it's in the blood!

SM: Did you encounter any prejudice in making such an offbeat choice?

AN: Yes. I remember, when I was leaving Cambridge in 1966, my supervisor in Cambridge told me that I was throwing away my career when I said that I was going to study in West Africa. He thought that I should go to some safe British University and look at old English and that sort of thing.

SM: That's interesting! What in your opinion are some of the major cultural changes happening in Britain today?

AN: Two things. One is the tremendous upsurge of interest in the multicultural scene to such an extent that you will find writers and artists complaining that they have been taken over by writers of the Caribbean, Asian, African and Chinese background. This has not worried me at all because I think Britain has always received cultures from outside and absorbed them within its own. The English language comes from so many different sources: Latin, Teutonic, Norman, and even in modern times, Hindi. Well, that ability to absorb other cultures once again shows itself very very strongly when we look at achievements of people like V.S. Naipaul, Salman Rushdie, Isigura, Carroll Philips, and indeed Winsome Pinnock, a Black playwright who has been accompanying us around India.

That is one of the big things. And the other, in fact, there arc two other things. One is the restatement of nationhood in Scotland, Wales, and to some extent, Northern Ireland, although the last is very complex because of political reasons; I should not get into them here. Particularly in Scotland and Wales, people are feeling that they are primarily Scottish or Welsh, and perhaps only secondarily British, and not English at all. So that is a very important thing. The third is that since the election of a new government in Britain in May 1997, there has been a remarkable sense of freshness of the nation perhaps entering not completely known but quite exciting new territory. Whether this is just images or reality, I must wait and see. But for the moment, the atmosphere in Britain is very positive and very energetic. I think people would say that, whatever they are politically. My family is largely Conservative. I come from the party that was defeated in the last election. Well, most of my family gave Tony Blair a chance because he is trying to do something to freshen up Britain. And I think a lot of people feel like that at the moment. It is a very positive mood after several years, in which, to be frank, there was a certain amount of despair.

SM: What are the implications of such cultural changes for those who happen to be in the field of literary studies?

AN: Well, I think it's impossible to teach literature now without taking note of the contemporary world. I am not talking of Britain. Probably because no part of the world's literature does not have a thriving contemporary literary scene because writers are the people who express feelings and nationalism, identity and those kinds of things and we in England have this exciting new energetic literature. I think for that reason you could not teach a course or study contemporary writing without taking note of the multicultural scene. I hope if you are teaching modern English literature, you would like to include some Scottish and Irish writers. So those changes I think are affecting literary studies.

SM: How do you, as Head of Literature of British Council, hope to address such changes within the U.K?

AN: One of the things that attracted me to my job is that my job description says that "I am to promote British and Commonwealth literature." You would have noticed that the British libraries in India stick to not just English, but also Scottish, Irish, Indian, Caribbean and Australian. Well, that is not in such quantities, but at least there is a recognition that the writing in English is promoted by the British Council. While in India I heard Jasper Utley, British Council, Chennai, say publicly that his job was to promote as much British writing in English as the Indian. And that is the view I entirely endorse. So here in India, I would hope to see the all-India seminars, such as the Lucknow seminar, take place every eighteen months or so, and other such initiatives.

SM: What specific measures are you contemplating in order to promote English studies outside Britain?

AN: I would like to see that kind of a seminar [the Lucknow kind] available to everyone. So that in whatever country you live, you are within reach of a seminar held annually that you could apply to. Obviously, we can only take a limited number to a seminar, although everyone would have the opportunity to apply.

If you would have lived in Europe, the Caribbean, Australia, wherever, there should be a seminar available with British writers and discussions with local writers. Secondly, I would like to see more emphasis on writers in residence. There is value in sending a team of writers. But there is much more value in letting a writer stay at a place for four to five weeks at least. And we have had a few examples of that with great success. I would like to try it here in India. Thirdly, I want to place much more emphasis on translation. British Council is at the centre of a unique worldwide cultural network and it is a lost opportunity if we do not promote translation between English and other languages both ways—from English into other languages, and from other languages into English. I hope that there will be an emphasis on this. And fourthly, the British Council is looking for ways in which it could bring new kinds of exhibitions promoting literature, perhaps using the Internet wherever it is available.

SM: What is your opinion about the language-literature debate? There are some who feel that they can teach language without bringing in literature.

AN: Yes, it is a debate that has gone on for so long. It is a false debate. It is like saying that we can survive without the head. I am not going to say which is the body and which is the head, but you cannot have literature without language and you cannot have language without literature. A person who uses language only for functional purposes is, in fact, quite ill-educated if they cannot read a book, a creative book, and has not seen language flower at its best. It is a very artificial thing to stop short of literature, just as I think those who read literature and stop short of understanding the language are missing a great deal. And so, I do not think the debate is a very valid one.

SM: How do you look at the question of identity politics that is going on not just in Britain but also in the U.S. and many other parts of the world?

AN: Well, I'm quite sympathetic to people trying to understand where they come from. We live in a world where a lot of people are feeling deracinated. They are in a migratory situation, I think. Therefore, having someone like Winsome Pinnock describe a journey back to Jamaica where her parents came from, although she was brought up in Britain, is very moving, and I can understand that. As Scotsmen, now people want to assert their Scottishness. At its worst, we see the effect in a place like Bosnia or Rwanda of that kind of an identity—nationalism that leads to negative forces. But at its best, it leads to cultural regeneration. My worry is that the so-called globalisation may not altogether be a good thing. We are producing a lot of trashy fiction that is available in all sorts of airport bookstores, hotel bookshops, and through the Internet. We are learning a common language that may not be of a very good quality. So there are a lot of counter forces to identity politics. Some people seem to have approved the move towards total globalisation. I am afraid a lot will be lost in the process.

SM: Identity politics at times produces divisiveness. It balkanises society. How can we prevent this?

AN: What you need is a balancing act. Rohinton Mistry, for instance, called his last novel *A Fine Balance*, and I would like to seek that fine balance, while proudly asserting the distinction of our own culture but not doing in a rabid or racist way. I think when you are so proud of your cultural background that you think it superior to anyone else's, that is very very dangerous. It is a better world when you respect other people's cultures.

SM: Are you happy with all the changes that are taking place in the field of literary studies? Can they be justified?

AN: Like what changes?

SM: For instance, some people like Alvin Kernan have announced the "death of literature."

AN: Yes. Somebody has also written a book called *The End of History.*

SM: And yet, Cleanth Brooks talks about the enduring value of the classics . . .

AN: Well, first of all, anyone who talks about the death of literature has no sense of history or understanding of human psychology or spirituality. It is impossible to conceive of the human race without literature. We cannot think of a situation when people have not wanted to express themselves through song, through poetry, and in modern times, through storytelling. The death of literature, I think, is a human impossibility. We may see genres of literature, categories of literature changes. You can legitimately question whether the novel, which was created for the leisured class in the eighteenth century, will have a future or not. I think it does. We see more and more novels published each year to prove that. But I think all such apocalyptic statements of the future of literature are very suspect.

SM: How did you get involved in D.H. Lawrence in the first place? What attracted you to him? And do you have the same interest in Lawrence now?

AN: Yes, indeed! Well, I have the same interest now, the same admiration for Lawrence as when I first read him. I think what attracted me to him was the feeling that he is the quintessential twentieth century man who recognised the dilemmas of living in the twentieth century. For all his dogmas, he is always questioning things. He is never in the end absolutely certain about anything, although his tone and voice might make him seem so. He is an inspiring figure because he questioned whether we should be as self-obsessed as the twentieth century has taught us. He also taught us that money, sex and material values do not really matter. He was constantly looking behind them, questioning spiritual things. He asked whether capitalism, science and modern industrialisation were the only roads down which we could go. Could we not learn something from the past? For instance, civilisations such as the Aztec, the Mexican. . . . He seems to be a very complex person. He is never the same in two different works. He was a provocative essayist, a brilliant letter writer, a competent poet. I am not sure whether I should put him in the first rank of poets. Some people would. And remember that he also painted. He is matched by very few people. In India, Rabindranath Tagore might be a parallel.

SM: And finally, what was your experience as a judge in the Commonwealth Literature prize?

AN: Well, the Commonwealth literature prize is difficult to administer because it has to be judged in all the Commonwealth countries. There are about fifty countries, clubbed into four regions. The Commonwealth Foundation in London administers this. I found it fascinating to be a judge in the final round where we could be looking at books from Canada, India and Nigeria and New Zealand . . . so you are really reaching across frontiers!

Theatre: Reaching out to People

Mahesh Dattani stands out in a group of high profile critics and writers. Acclaimed as a leading playwright in English, he has now bagged the Sahitya Akademi Award for English Literature for his play Final Solutions. *In an interview with me, the playwright-director spoke of his art and the state of theatre in India.*

Excerpts from the Interview

SM: How and when did you start writing plays?

MD: I began writing plays about ten years ago. It is an interesting story because I never really set out to be a playwright. I think very few say that they wish to be a playwright initially. I was involved in the theatre from a very young age, in the sense that although I didn't participate, I was attracted to the theatre.

SM: Where did you receive your early education?

MD: In Baldwins School, Bangalore. Later, I studied at St. Joseph's College where I read History, Economics, Political Science. My interest in theatre sort of grew side by side in college. I became a member of a popular amateur theatre company called the "Bangalore Little Theatre." I used to do a lot of work such as backstage acting and stuff like that. Later, I moved on to directing plays.

SM: Can you mention some names?

MD: Yes. I did Sartre's play translated as *In Camera* and I produced the effect of Gama rays in *The Man of the Moon*. Then an American play—all-female cast. Subsequently, I started my own theatre company and my first production was Hipolytes by Euripides. That didn't go down too well for various reasons. Next, I did a few comedies. Really lighthearted. At that point, I felt the need to do plays, Indian plays in English language. I wasn't entirely happy with the translation available, I felt that the language was stilted. It just didn't present any real speech; it was either far too academic or just did a literal translation of the original. So I felt that there ought to be more plays written originally in the English language. I decided to try my hand at it. That's how I began writing. After the first play, there has been no looking back. People accepted me. And as a result of doing Indian plays, my audience actually grew.

SM: What was your first play?

MD: It's called *Where There's a Will* and it's about this patriarch who controls his family—his wife, son and daughter-in-law. He dies at the end of the first scene, and his ghost becomes the narrator. What he has done is that he has left a very convoluted "Will" and his family had to act according to his wishes to inherit. The ghost is later exorcised by the women.

SM: Excellent! Now, Mahesh, drama as a genre is, in a sense, not very popular. At the same time, it remains one of the most powerful mediums. How does it feel to handle such a genre?

MD: Well, I think this is a wrong perception prevailing among the academics, especially the view that writing for the stage is inferior to writing a novel or writing poetry. I think it is important to keep in mind that the playwright is actually a craftsman. He is a "wright" and not "write." Sorry if I'm pontificating . . .

SM: Not at all! Please go on.

MD: Well, I think it's more to do really with dramatic structure and less with literary skills. I think the skill of the playwright is listening to day-to-day speech and not making it sound flowery. At least I try to be different. I think it has more to do with understanding human relationships and how conflict can be presented on stage. I don't see it as less popular. For instance, even a serious play like *Final Solutions* had about forty shows in Bombay.

SM: Extraordinary!

MD: Yes. Maybe 25-30,000 people saw it. Now, I'm not sure what the readership of a novel in India would be!

SM: Okay. Looking back, Mahesh, what do you think have been your major achievements?

MD: I don't know whether I've had any significant achievements.

SM: You know you've been well received by the public that appreciates good theatre.

MD: Well, maybe the sheer fact that I'm projecting a milieu that is close to the audience—I think that may itself be an achievement. That's what makes my theatre alive.

SM: Can you remember some names of the plays that have become more successful?

MD: I think *Dance Like a Man* and *Tara* are the two plays that have been commercially the most successful.

SM: A few words about each of them.

MD: Okay! *Dance Like a Man*, this is during my Bharatanatyam days. It is about an old couple, dancers, ex-dancers. They are in their sixties and they are looking back at the past when they struggled against the stigma attached to Bharatanatyam in the fifties, that it was a *devadasi's* dance, compounding the problem for the man.

Tara is about a boy and girl, Siamese twins. I have taken medical liberty over here because Siamese twins are invariably of the same sex and they are surgically separated at birth. It was important for their survival and the play deals with their emotional separation.

SM: How do you look at the Anglo-American theatre in this country? The theatre that has been traditionally presented in the English departments? Do you think such plays have any social or cultural relevance today?

MD: This definitely seems to be a problem. People get very upset when I say this. I think that this kind of cultural imitation reflects more a feeling of inferiority among the people who do it. I've been a victim of that as well. It's that you aspire to belong to a culture that is really not yours; it can never be yours. The cultural aspiration is actually projected by the way one does Anglo-American plays. I think it has nothing to do with theatre, it is a personal aspiration, a sad reflection of what kind of culture we value. We don't see this as any different from colonial inferiority. It's definitely a throw-back on that. However, that does not negate the fact that there are people who are doing very good work using European or American plays.

SM: Would it, therefore, be accurate to describe the choice you've made in the field of Indian theatre as part of decolonisation?

MD: Again, I don't think I had such lofty political ideals when I began writing. I think it was a personal discovery because I too grew up with missionary or convent education. Of course, I was told that our art and culture were inferior to European culture. And there was a rebel in me, you know. I stopped reading Yeats and Shakespeare for a long time because I felt that I had enough of such stuff during my school days. I made an attempt to understand myself better and I guess this prompted me to do Indian plays.

SM: Mahesh, you have always attempted to depict in your plays the themes and concerns of everyday experience. What motivated you to take up such an approach?

MD: Well, again perhaps this is a projection of who I am. In America, playwrights are searching for things to talk about because everything has been done, and the audience has become blasé. But what is interesting here is that the blasé attitude is not there among the audience. I think there is so much happening today—gender equation and class consciousness, for instance.

SM: What have been the modes that you have chosen for yourself? Has it always been the realistic mode, or have you attempted other modes such as the expressionistic, or the mythological, for instance?

MD: Again, I think the use of myths or legends has its own problems because you already have a mindset towards that. So what invariably might happen is that if you see yourself as a radical, you would try to pass an antithesis to popular myths or legends. Hopefully not? Or sometimes you might just project the same values that are there, knowingly or unknowingly. Supposing you did a play like the *Liberation of Sita*, it amounts to sacrilege. And as for the other forms, I think it has a lot to do with the context.

As for realism, this may be true. I think realism is one of the forms that I use. Because of its popularity in the West, it continues to be relevant. It has got a new lease of life due to television. Playwrights are writing realistic scripts for the stage in order to get accepted. I see realism as one of the forms that I've made use of. I've used the chorus as a narrative device, and I've used time and space in different ways in my plays. I think all the tools of theatre are available to a playwright and you just use them the way your sensibility allows you to use them.

SM: Who has had a major influence on your art?

MD: Well, I was particularly impressed by the plays of Vijay Tendulkar. Actually, that was one of the reasons why I decided to write myself, because when I saw plays in Hindi or Gujarati and I managed to acquire the translation, they just didn't have the same impact. *Silence, the Court is in Session!* was such a brilliant play, but I felt that the translation in English threw away most of the effect. Later on, it was Tennessee Williams. I relate to Tennessee Williams because he writes about vulnerable women in a very violent society. I think I tend to do that as well, although I don't see my woman as vulnerable, in the sense that they do fight their battles. They are not on the winning side of the battle, and I think I have learnt a lot about dramatic structure.

SM: What has been your understanding of Gujarati plays? I understand that Gujarati is your mother tongue. I'm sure that you had some acquaintance with Gujarati theatre. What would you think is the current stage of Gujarati theatre and how do you relate it to Marathi theatre?

MD: It's like chalk and cheese. I feel that Marathi theatre is far more sophisticated and in the mainstream, whereas Gujarati theatre tends to be classic. Gujarati theatre has a very strong following; Marathi has no less, but the kind of stuff that is put on the Gujarati stage leaves a lot to be desired. I won't even call some of it as theatre.

SM: Slapstick?

MD: Even if it was slapstick well done, I think that would be good theatre. It's just that it's a very weak plot; most of it is just plagiarised West-End or Broadway sex comedy. They throw in a lot of topical jokes, and there is no dramatic effect. I don't think the audience is looking for that. It's just melodrama blue. At the worst, it is just a series of blue jokes. I think the only group that's doing something worthwhile, perhaps, is the Indian National Theatre, where they do Marathi and Gujarati plays. They have a long tradition of being slightly more political. They have revived Bhavai and done some interesting things. The rest of it, at least to my knowledge, is pure junk. Some of the good stuff that has come out of Gujarati theatre like *Gandhi Virodh Gandhi* are actually adaptations of the original Marathi plays. The good stuff is from the Marathi theatre.

SM: How did you conceive of a play like *The Final Solutions*, which is based on the issue of fundamentalism, and in particular, the destruction of Babri Masjid? How did you think of it?

MD: Well, I wrote the plays before the destruction of the Babri Masjid, when the Ram Janma Bhoomi was an issue in Parliament. I was commissioned to write that play by Alyque Padamsee. Initially I was hesitant.

SM: What is the main structural outline of the play?

MD: It's about two Muslim boys running away from a mob and seeking shelter in a Hindu household. Now, it transpires that they know the girl who lives there. The prejudices of the family are brought to the forefront. There is, of course, a façade of being liberal-minded.

SM: The Third Reich and the Holocaust! Is that where the title came from?

MD: Yes, exactly!

SM: Mahesh, how do you look at the current state of the Indian-English theatre?

MD: Well, there definitely is more prolific maturity in the cities. Some of it good and some bad. . . . However, there is now a definite focus on Indian plays that try to embody the kind of values and aspirations I've been talking about. I do see this effort as breaking fresh ground. There is more money in English language theatre than in any other theatre in the country, and I feel that it is moving in the right direction. Again, the problem is how to maintain a standard—because almost all the English language theatre in our country is amateur; very few people actually have formal training. I think that's what we need to focus on now.

SM: What do you think can be done to make theatre more accessible to the people?

MD: Unless you reflect the ethos of the people, it is going to be an elitist theatre; or it is going to be a museum piece intended to satisfy curiosity. On the other hand, if you widen your audience, the only thing you can do is to write more about them.

SM: What are your views about the patronage of the theatre in India by business houses that, of course, have their own interests?

MD: Well, it's a mixed blessing. In a sense, there is more money available. There are strings attached, no doubt! You have to do something that they feel is right for the image of the company. It's like taking one step forward and two steps backward. The money is available and so we feel there is a chance to do more theatre. You are taking two steps backward because the kind of theatre you are doing, for instance, say . . .

SM: Neil Simon comedies?

MD: Yes. Or a musical like *My Fair Lady*. I don't see the point in doing that. I think the corporate houses need to look at their own images. They are anxious to project a Westernised image. That way, they are losing the market. The successful ones are those that have captured the national spirit. Just look at the "Hamara Bajaj" ad, for instance. It might be corny, but it captures the sentiment of the masses. Then there are the other corporate houses, the banks and the mobiles, for instance. I think it's quite stupid—if they want to capture a wider section of the market, they have to reflect its ethos. Unfortunately, in the advertising field, at the top of the corporate world, people have a . . .

SM: Western mindset?

MD: Yes, exactly! It's silly. It's bad marketing policy, really.

SM: Although you are eminently qualified, you have chosen to be a freelancer. Do you find this situation congenial for your creative work?

MD: You know, to the theatre practitioner, it's a full-time job. You have to be mad to be able to do it! Maybe I have that kind of madness because I could easily be doing something boring and earning a lot. But then, would that not kill me?

"A Good Translation is a Good Literary Text"

Translation is like a lifeline that not only passes information but also changes the sensibility, and is judged in the same way as any other literary text. Translators, who are not bound by rules but ethics, need to look into the lesser-known languages to communicate to a wider spectrum. This comes out in a conversation with Professor Kuhiwczak.

Piotr Kuhiwczak (pronounced Kuhichak) is the Director of the Centre for British and Comparative Cultural Studies at Warwick University, Convetry, U.K. He has had wide experience in teaching translation, English and European literatures and cultural studies. Among the important conferences on translation that he organised or co-organised are the 1986 BCLA conference on *Shakespeare and Translation* (Warwick) and the 1988 international conference *Beyond Translation* (Warwick). Dr. Kuhiwczak took time off from the 1996 Warwick seminar on literary translation and spoke to me, fellow-participant in the seminar, on translation, ideology, culture and related issues.

Excerpts from the Interview

SM: Why do you think Translation Studies is increasingly gaining ground as an influential discipline worldwide?

PK: Yes, indeed, the discipline of translation has been growing rapidly in the past 15-20 years. The underlying fact that we are dealing with here is easy communication. It's much easier to communicate with people across big spaces. Travel, Internet, telephone, faxes—these increase the possibility of communication. At the same time, it is true that we speak many different languages. And so, at one end, there is globalisation, and at the other there is interest in the cultures of other people. However, the fact that people speak English does not mean that they are in some ways English and American peoples; they have their own culture. I think confronting the other culture is interesting, and people try to do this constantly.

SM: While translation invades every aspect of our daily life, a paradoxical fact is that literature and humanities programmes in the universities do not have translation courses in the core curriculum. Why is it so?

PK: Yes, it's true all over the place, with some good exceptions. I don't fully understand the reason. It's a mystery to me. But if translation courses are not included in most cases in modern language degrees, the idea is to study foreign cultures and foreign languages separately, and that addresses the issue. Translation is like going to another country, pretending to be in a country other than one's own. I think the resistance to translation is a very negative phenomenon. Perhaps it's the time now for change. There is a chance that something will change in the old-fashioned departments soon.

SM: Is the resistance on account of orthodoxy and exclusivity that you find in many disciplines?

PK: Yes, I think it is so. Or it may be the need to preserve the status quo and the security it offers, because then you don't have to question anything. You don't need to change anything; you sort of go along on well-established lines and pretend that you don't see any change of avenue.

SM: Let me take you to a slightly different area—the debate in *The Times Literary Supplement* (13 October 1995) between Timothy Buck and Lawrence Vinuti over Helen Lowe Porter's translation of Thomas Mann suggests the extent to which ignorance persists even in so-called informed circles about the fidelity-betrayal syndrome supposedly underlying all translation activity. What do you think explains the persistence of such a view for so long in literary circles?

PK: I think if you're dealing with literary circles, you are dealing with people who don't translate. They are, for instance, reading the texts in their own languages and since this is the Anglo-American context, reading translations is not the standard procedure. People don't read that many translations. A monolingual person does not usually understand the mechanics of language and culture. People still believe that there is some "faithful" translation that should be produced. But when you ask them, they don't exactly know what we should be "faithful" to. So it's a very general concept.

SM: Yet in the history of translation, there have been significant exceptions . . .

PK: Oh, yes, there have been many exceptions. The problem I think is that something went wrong with Europe in the nineteenth century, because if you look before the nineteenth century, there was very little conviction in the fidelity concept. Fidelity was understood in a very different way. Let me make use of a classic example, Alexander Pope's translation of *Iliad* into English. In terms of the common understanding of *Iliad*, there is no fidelity at all. It's actually called rewriting of the *Iliad*. It is Pope's own interpretation put into heroic couplets. Pope made his own decisions regarding what should go and what would not be understood. What he does is also very interesting. He explains in the Preface and in the footnote what he is doing. He is producing the translation that is not faithful and he is telling you the reason. The nineteenth century glossed it over.

SM: What could have been the cultural reasons?

PK: The cultural reasons are two. One reason is partly academic. It has to do with the rapid development in philology—the study of languages, contrastive study of languages, and the belief that you have always the corresponding word in another language. This is not true. So that's one reason. The second reason is the very strong belief in the nineteenth century that language is very much spiritually connected to the culture of ethnic groups. So if you take this assumption, then you don't want to discuss about translation in terms of what is lost and gained because what you are talking about is the integrity of the value of these people who produce the text. Producing the translation not faithful in the classic technique was really very unacceptable at that time. Unfortunately, we are still to a great extent in the nineteenth century mould.

SM: In the "Translator's Invisibility" (1995, London & Routledge), Lawrence Vinuti introduces two important concepts called foreignisation and domestication. In what ways do these terms advance our thinking on the subject?

PK: Well, it depends on what you understand as foreignisation and domestication. I think that every good translation that is accepted in a way deals with the process of domestication. It is not clear as to whether Vinuti is talking about attitudes or about procedures. Now, I think that foreignisation is possible, but it depends on what level you do it. If you do it at the level of language only, then you manipulate the structure in a particular way so that the readers are sure that there is a certain description.

I am not talking here about the academic reader, I am talking here about the average educated person who goes to the shop and buys the book to enjoy it. This will be turned down, I think, in every culture. I don't think that Indian culture is the exception. But if you look at the question of translating the text from one of the Indian languages into English spoken in India, it sounds different to the English speaker from Britain. Well, if it is done, I can't see any reason why it can't be accepted. Of course, then do you call it foreignisation or domestication? I would call it domestication. . . . The argument is that the British reader accepts the English spoken in India and the artistic way it is dealt with. Once they accept it, they domesticate it. It is not foreign any more because it enters the convention, the literary site of the target culture.

SM: Piotr, do you believe that translation activities are the necessary part of cultural practice everywhere? In what significant sense?

PK: Well, the obvious reason why I think it is an inter-language communication is similar to intra-language communication. What is new in it is the cultural input. And indeed, this is necessary. You can't think about somebody who is educated or claims to be educated if he/she is monocultural. I mean, being monocultural is very dangerous because it is not what it means. To be monocultural is not to allow for the other possibilities. So yes, translation is a very important exercise.

SM: The view that the translator is a second-rate creator and an imitator can be traced back to the romantic/modernist concept of the creative process, and yet there is the opposite view that literary translations are original and even more challenging. In what sense do they pose a greater creative challenge?

PK: I think that a good literary translation is very difficult to achieve, as the creative process is very complex. It is not easy to write well. But it is very difficult to translate well because there is a certain discipline you deal with. There is the original text. This is something with which you are fighting in one way or another, but it's still there. Whether you make a domesticated translation or you foreignise the translation, the text is still there. And what you want to achieve at the end of the day is your translations. It is supposed to be wholly judged, like the original text. It will either stand along the original text or it will not stand. It's a very difficult task.

SM: How does translation become a shaping force for literary change and development? How does it introduce new concepts, forms and genres in literary systems?

PK: It is a very complex, social and cultural phenomenon. I would say that the target culture accepts novelty only when it is a ready force. I don't think there is any way one can impose any innovation on the receiving culture. And at different historical periods, the cultures go through changes. Sometimes, they close to the outside world and open. And there is a need to borrow from other cultures. And in this sense, translation is like a lifeline because it is not only passing information, it is changing the sensibility as well. It hasn't been explained exactly why certain genres enter certain cultures, in particular historical times rather than other times.

But that's what happens, and if you follow the development of the genres and look at different cultures, you can see that's how they develop, through borrowing. The culture borrows the genre and develops it. You can look at the nineteenth-century Russian novel. I mean, the novel was not originally a Russian genre; it was borrowed from Western Europe. The Russians developed it and in a way re-exported it to Western Europe after reshaping it. So, it's a sort of reciprocal arrangement that happened. I would call these situations miracles. And they happened. We don't fully understand why.

SM: Excellent! So you think there should be an ethic for a translation? Is there a right way of translating a text? What do you think are the responsibilities of an ideal translator?

PK: I believe there are ethical questions. They are always there. Ideally, one would believe that the translator should be responsible. Not only for the way he/she translates, but for the consequences of his translation. Once again, it depends as to what text we are talking about. If you take the history of the Bible translation in Europe, you can see that the whole exercise was not about language at all, it was about beliefs. And you could see that throughout the late Middle Ages, the Renaissance period, people were actually losing their heads over the translations of the Bible because it was the issue of doctrine that we are talking about. We don't have to deal with questions like this very often. With writing, sometimes yes, but not with translation.

However, I think translators should understand the issue and what they need is the knowledge of translation history, what responsibilities are carried with the text they translate. Of course, in the modern world with so much literature of the popular kind, you know that the book is written in London and is translated into languages. It does not matter how it is translated. People read it. In this case, I don't think any rules or any ethical questions will matter. I think it is like that, it's very difficult to apply rules to all cases.

SM: You have a Polish background. Perhaps you'd like to talk about translation as a site of political resistance?

PK: It's a very interesting question. I remember that during the Communist regime, there was a system of censorship of original texts and translation. Poland, being the centre of Europe, enjoyed a very central position. In the forty-year period of Soviet domination, you'd see that translation was a very important part of the illegal underground publishing. If you manage to get texts translated and received, and know that your private thoughts have been made public in another country in writing, you then start thinking that you might be right.

And whatever you hear of being told to you on television and radio would not be true. That is why translation was crucial in undermining the servitude of the Communist regime. Texts were always perceived differently. For instance, George Orwell's *Animal Farm* in Britain was perceived as a commentary on the BBC or the position of the Left. In Eastern Europe, that was a metaphor for the Communist system. The text was hunted by the Secret Police. And that is the great power of a translated text.

Partition Revisited

Hindus and Muslims, Pakistan and India, need to come to some kind of understanding of each other's cultures. Therefore, the novel ought to have a new meaning for readers fifty years after the subcontinent was divided. In this conversation, Shiv K. Kumar speaks to me on the theme of partition.

Poet, novelist, short story writer, playwright, translator, critic and educationist, Shiv K. Kumar has had a distinguished career in India and abroad. An eminent Indian-English poet, Dr. Kumar has six collections of poetry to his credit. He has also published two novels *The Bone's Prayer* and *Nude Before God*, a play, a translation of the Pakistani poet Faiz Ahmed Faiz, and several scholarly works.

In 1978, Shiv K. Kumar was elected a Fellow of the Royal Society of Literature (FRSL), London, and in 1988 he received the Central Sahitya Akademi Award for his collection of poems *Trapfalls in the Sky*. In 1991, *The Journal of South Asian Literature*, Michigan, USA, brought out a special issue on him. In 1998, Kumar published a Partition novel, *A River with Three Banks: The Partition of India: Agony and Ecstasy* (New Delhi: UBS Publishers).

A Punjabi born in Lahore, Kumar came to India in 1947. Traumatised by the experience of the holocaust, he decided to write a fictionalised account years later, he says, in order to exorcise the ghost of Partition from his being.

In this interview, Shiv K. Kumar talks to me about his compulsions to write the novel, the moral vision of *A River with*

Three Banks, his views on the art of the novel, his self-assessment as a poet and a translator, and the importance of creative writing as he sees it, in a world increasingly sold to computers and cybernetics.

Excerpts from the Interview

SM: Congratulations on your new novel *A River with Three Banks*. May I begin by asking you as to what prompted you to write a Partition novel?

SK: The reason is very simple. I myself am a migrant from Pakistan. I was born in Lahore and I migrated to Delhi in 1947 when the communal holocaust was at its worst. You know, every Punjabi writer has to get the trauma of the Partition out of his system sooner or later. Now, I could have written the novel a few years after the Partition, as Khushwant Singh did when he wrote *A Train to Pakistan* in 1952. There were other Punjabi writers who wrote on the same theme—C.L. Nahal, Bhisham Sahni and Kartar Singh Duggal. I believe in what Wordsworth said, that "a poem is emotion recollected in tranquillity." An emotion has to be recollected and recaptured after a passage in time so that you have a better understanding of your experience. If you are too close to the canvas of your painting, you can't see it in the proper perspective. You have to stand back a little from the canvas. I had to stand fifty years back from 1947.

SM: Okay, the business of capturing the experience in tranquillity is fine; it's just that we don't live in tranquil times right now! On the other hand, as I see it, this fact, negative as it is, might suggest a certain truth. Because we are currently debating the notion of nationhood and the folly of Partition, perhaps now is the time to write a novel about Partition. What do you think?

SK: Absolutely! Actually, I think my novel has an urgent contemporary relevance because the communal situation in India is still the same as in 1947. Hindus and Muslims, Pakistan and India, need to come to some kind of understanding of each other's cultures. Therefore, the novel ought to have a new meaning for readers fifty years after the subcontinent was divided.

SM: What is your opinion of some of the major Indian novels dealing with the theme of Partition? Who do you think has had seminal influence upon you?

SK: I'd say that I was not directly influenced by any of these novelists. Each Punjabi novelist has his own story to tell. As for me, I knew that I had come to terms with the fact of Partition. There are certain common symbols and metaphors, though. For instance, Khushwant Singh uses the train metaphor in his *A Train to Pakistan*. Several short stories of Bhisham Sahni also bring in the train and the journey motif. In the last part of my novel, there is a train journey from Delhi to Amritsar. The train is waylaid and ambushed by Hindu fanatics on the way. Thus, for me, it is a journey from one country to another, from one point of view to another, from one way of life to another, and from the known to the unknown, with the train and the river as primary symbols.

SM: Of all the Partition novels I have read, this is perhaps one of the most vivid portrayals of the trauma of Partition. In your account, you seem to blend the religious and political themes very well. Your character Gautam Mehta is born a Hindu, becomes a Christian for expediency, and then embraces Islam when he falls in love with a Muslim girl. Is this some form of liberal humanism? Do you think this is an accurate description of your position in the novel?

SK: Indeed! I think every religion basically advocates brotherhood, compassion, understanding and love. The essence of all religion is unity. It is only the outward façade, the ritual, the orthodoxy in each religion that differentiates. Therefore Gautam Mehta, a liberal humanist, a man with creative sensibility, sees no barriers whatsoever. No doubt he sees Christianity as a ploy to get divorce. The conversion certificate, he knows, is a passport to release him from an estranged marriage from a wife who has been unfaithful to him. When he falls in love with Haseena, her mother tells him that he has to convert to Islam. Gautam sees no problem in that because he is in love and love recognises no barriers. He is not looking at Haseena as a Muslim girl but as a human being, as a young girl of rare sensitivity, compassion, understanding and commitment to human values. When the novel ends, Haseena asks: "Would I now be Mrs. Gautam Mehta?" Gautam says, "No, you would always remain Haseena. We'll start a new race and we'll call it Gautam Haseena. This is how the new generation will begin—sans nationality, sans religion, sans language, sans any kind of barriers." Towards the end, I've described the flight of birds. To my mind, they represent an utter indifference to man-made barriers. From where they fly, they seem to be scornful of happenings on earth when men are at each other's throats.

SM: In celebrating such unity underlying religions, aren't you underplaying the reservations that many minority faiths have in their desire to retain their uniqueness of approach? For instance, Gautam's father Shyamlal describes Christ as an Indian yogi or a prophet. Isn't this tendency at the so-called appropriation or "assimilation" that some minority religions resent vis-à-vis Hinduism?

SK: I'd say that these members of the minority community who may resent these attempts at building bridges must be hard-boiled fanatics attached to their religions. But there are liberal-minded people in all religions such as the Frontier Gandhi, Khan Abdul Gaffar Khan, and Abul Kalam Azad. My character, Shyamlal, is an orthodox Arya Samajist. You will kindly remember that in Lahore, he used to address rallies in which he would debunk the Christian missionaries. But in his case, a subtle change comes about in his heart because of his indulgent love of his son. So when he wants to pick up the conversion certificate from Father Jones, he remarks that Christ's resurrection could have a Hindu explanation, that like a Hindu yogi who could remain buried underground without the loss of his limbs, Christ too had controlled his breathing system.

Similarly, when Gautam falls in love and marries Haseena, he begins to read the Koran, and in one of the sermons delivered by Prophet Mohammed, he discovers that all mankind is one family and that God sends His messengers as bearers of good tidings who come to earth to punish evil and reward virtue. Shyamlal at that point says: "Doesn't that sound like Lord Krishna?" Now, some Muslims could feel offended that Prophet Mohammed has been built into an *avatar*. I believe that would be an utter misunderstanding of a point of view that in fact raises the Prophet to a great pedestal.

SM: In another context, you said that if only the literary artists in India had anticipated the nightmarish consequences of the Partition, perhaps the calamity could have been avoided. But given the communal polarisation that existed during the forties in India, don't you think that this is largely a matter of wishful thinking?

SK: As a writer, I'd like to indulge, if you permit me, in such wishful thinking. For instance, there were some writers and visionaries who never accepted the Partition even when the terms and conditions were being negotiated. Take, for example, Gandhiji who was a prophet and a loner. Or take the writer, Sadat Hasan Manto, whose story is one of the most outstanding of our times. In *Toba Tek Singh*, he ironically suggests that it was only the mad Toba Singh who in a Pakistani mental asylum refuses to accept the reality of the Partition. Now, it is a madman, as it were, who understands that you cannot thrive or flourish on division. Sometimes, it is such people who strike one as being more balanced than those who belong to the so-called normal rungs of humanity.

The other day, I was told that [Pakistani Prime Minister] Nawaz Sharif's native village was actually in India. When he became the Prime Minister, the villagers apparently celebrated in the form of a special ceremony that one of the sons of the soil had attained such success. Similarly, I.K. Gujral was born in Sialkot, and the school that he went to felt very proud of his attainment when he became the Prime Minister. There are many such movements of compassion, love and understanding. When you become a politician, you think only in terms of differences. It is only the artists who manage to overcome differences.

SM: In your novel, one finds that the personal crisis of the protagonist Gautam Mehta gets intersected with the crisis in the history of the nation. How did you think of this interesting plot? Does it have any basis in fact?

SK: I guess you want to know whether there are autobiographical elements in the novel. Absolutely none. You see, there are two kinds of experiences that a writer uses. One can be his personal, limited, intimate experience, and the other is the vicarious experience of his friends. Now, I know of several instances where people have got married to abducted Muslim girls, just as several Muslims who came to India fell in love with Hindu girls. I wove some of these experiences of the people I knew into the story. The only portrait of a real character in the novel is that of Shyamlal Mehta, who is modelled after my father who was an Arya Samajist. Of course, I have made Shyamlal a very ingenious person who even manipulates his own thinking to suit the convenience of his son.

SM: In one of the episodes of the novel, you seem to make an equation between the pimp and the politician. The common point between the two is quite obvious. Both are mercenary and both make use of people. Yet, your characters such as Gautam, Haseena or Berry, Gautam's friend, cannot escape the snare of the pimp or the politician.

SK: You have made me conscious of something in the novel that I had done but was not quite aware of. There is obviously something common between pimps and some of our politicians. [There are good politicians too!] But the hard fact is that most of our politicians are corrupt, they are after power. In the same manner, pimps like Pannalal are blindly after a share of the profit and therefore push the helpless Haseena into prostitution. The interesting thing is that among the pimps, there are no religious barriers. Pannalal, a Hindu, works in collaboration with Suleman Ghani, a Muslim. Both are partners in this nefarious business of selling abducted girls.

SM: What is the rationale of the title *A River with Three Banks*?

SK: What I had in mind was three religions. The relationship between Gautam and Haseena was consummated through three religions. Gautam, a Hindu, becomes a Christian in order to get his divorce, and then accepts Islam to marry Haseena. So these three religions in a sense are the three banks of the river—a sort of confluence that brings Gautam and Haseena together.

There is another line of interpretation that can be seen. Pannalal gets killed on the banks of the Ganga, which is also the confluence of Yamuna and Saraswati.

SM: What could be the possible evocation of Saraswati here?

SK: Gautam being a rationalist does not believe in Saraswati, but as a creative person, his imagination gets stimulated. Even the Allahabad fort, I am told, is three-faceted. It was, as I understand, built by Ashoka and then renovated by Akbar, and it was this fort where a Christian garrison was massacred during the Great Uprising in 1857.

SM: And yet a reader astutely pointed out that there is a third dimension and that is the sky common to people across the border. Also, the birds that fly admit no political frontiers.

SK: Yes, indeed, this is a fascinating interpretation that Dr. C. Rangarajan, Governor of Andhra Pradesh, offered when he released the book here in Hyderabad.

SM: The colour of the Saraswati river is described as white in the novel. What is the significance?

SK: White suggests purity. Clearly, the element of purity is entirely lacking in contemporary India. We seem to live with all kinds of impurities—religious, financial and moral.

SM: Poetry- and Partition-revisited literature seem to be taking a back seat everywhere. How does a creative writer rehabilitate art to its sacred status?

SK: The prophet of our time is Bill Gates, the software prophet. Even in India, young men are moving towards computer software and business management. Western capitalism is the latest manna from heaven!

As for me, I am allergic to electronic gadgets. I've even a poem in my sixth collection of poems, *Wool Gatherers*, in which I see the green screen of the computer hiding a cat that might leap out and scratch my face. Now, creativity is at the other end of the spectrum. I am reminded of what Sir James Jean said in his book *The Mysterious Universe*, that if half a dozen monkeys were to keep jumping up and down on the keyboard of a typewriter (that was before the days of computers), they will never be able to create a single sonnet of Shakespeare! Permutations and combinations will not help! I wish more of our universities would offer courses in creative writing. I wish philosophy was rehabilitated. However, the present scenario is not entirely bleak. I find that the younger generation expresses itself far more creatively than many members of my generation.

SM: At an age when most people would call it a day, you refuse to quit. What's your next novel going to be?

SK: My next novel is tentatively called *The Third Eye*. You might say that it will be an Indo-Cambridge novel because I draw upon my Cambridge experience. Once again, there is a quest for truth, with death as a primary motif, from where you look for the meaning of existence. In addition, I am already into the seventh collection of poems . . .

Creating an Alternative Universe

My words are the confused nightingale's half-lost, half-dead song at Spring's end, my language is the deaf mute infant's hands, eternally outstretched towards the angel's unknown quarters: its cry embossed on the earth's sun-baked face

From the poem "Words"

Modern Orissa's leading and best known poet, Sitakant Mahapatra was educated at Utkal, Allahabad and Cambridge Universities. He holds a doctorate in Social Anthropology, and was a member of the Indian Administrative Service.

Dr. Mahapatra has a substantial body of works to his credit—twelve collections of poetry, four volumes of essays in Oriya, four collections of translations, nine collections of tribal poetry translated into English, and more than ten critical essays in English.

Dr. Mahapatra spoke to me about his self-assessment as a poet, his translations of the poetry of the Indian tribes, his future plans, and related issues.

Excerpts from the Interview

SM: It is said that poets are born, not made. What is your self-assessment as a poet?

MA: Well, I think that poets are both born and made at the same time. There must be a certain quality of the mind, a quality of the imagination, a special way of looking at the reality that is, to an extent, latent within a poet. But like the sharpening of the instrument of an artisan, a poet too has to constantly sharpen his attitude or his way of using language, the way he has to formulate his themes and adopt a particular style for a particular theme. All these are parts of a kind of practice. Therefore, to an extent, he is also made. I do not believe that poets can be made if they do not have any talent. That is why I am very suspicious of poetry classes where poetry is taught. Poetry writing cannot be taught, but surely poets who have the inherent talent can learn from others by their own reading. By coming into contact with other fellow poets and by reading poetry, they can sharpen their own intellect.

SM: When did you first start writing poetry?

MA: It was when I was at Ravenshaw College. It must have been around 1957-58. I came to the college in 1953. Between 1953-55, I was editing the Ravenshaw College journal, and I had written some pieces—some editorials as well as some articles and a couple of poems. But from 1957 onwards, I think, I started publishing poems in the literary pages of newspapers like *Prajatantra* and other newspapers. The poems written between 1957-62 got into my first anthology, which was published in 1963. It was called *Dipti O Dwiti* (*The Flame and the Illumination*).

SM: Why did you decide to join the Administrative Service?

MA: Well, that's now a long story as I look back. Mine has been a generation of teachers in the family, beginning with my great-grandfather. They were all teachers. I too had started with a good academic background and career. I started teaching after my post-graduation at Allahabad University. Then I stood first in the all-India competition in the IAS. I consulted my father and some of my teachers at Allahabad. My father said, "Well, I'm told that times are changing and that even if you are in the service, you can also continue your interest in literature and the arts. But if you don't accept the service, you can't get back to it. You can always leave the service if you wished to. Whatever it is, one advice I would give you is don't get uneducated! Now, that advice I hope I have followed.

SM: How is that you have been drawn to poetry alone and no other genres of literature?

MA: Poetry comes to me naturally, I must say. Other genres of literature I somehow have not tried. Of course, I have handled literary poetical matters through essays, non-literary critical articles. But my confrontation with reality, the way I look at my own experiences relating to love, to remorse, death, all these find appropriate expression through the poetic language. And that is why poetry has come as a natural medium to me.

SM: Many critics have said that your poetry is strongly rooted in the local myth, colour and sensibility? How do you manage to combine the regional sensibility with the modern Western temper?

MA: Well, I grew up in an atmosphere of intense love for classical Oriya poetry as well as Sanskrit poetry. My father was very well versed in all that had gone into the making of modern Oriya poetry, right from the Bhagavata, the Ramayana and the Mahabharata in the Oriya language, and the Sanskrit classics of poetry like Kalidasa or Bhavabhuti. He was extremely fluent in both Sanskrit as well as Oriya. I could often see that he would recite them from memory. That was very inspiring to me. That is where I absorbed an influence. I also learned from the oral tradition of Harivansa and the other Puranas. No doubt, to these were later on added my own readings of European, British and American poetry. I looked at the way some of these poets have been using language and how different it was from the way our poets looked at reality. The use of language seemed to articulate a particular kind of thought. In a way, two streams entered into me—the local classical tradition of poetry in my own language and in Sanskrit, besides the Anglo-European and the American tradition of poetry in which more than the British, more than the English poets, I owe a greater debt to the Spanish and the French.

SM: Some critics have found a strong influence of poets like Eliot. Is this true?

MA: *Wasteland* and *Four Quartets* had certainly influenced me and my generation at one time. We thought this was the approach to poetry; the use of mythological structure was perhaps appropriate. But then we got over Eliot. Guru Prasad Mohanty of my time wrote a very long poem, *Kala Purusha*. Ramakanth Rath, myself and others were certainly influenced by the strong use of archetypes and myths that Eliot used. But then we grew beyond it. As I said earlier, there has been a greater influence of Spanish poets like Lorca and French poets like Baudelaire and Rambau, for instance.

SM: In what ways?

MA: It is perhaps the way the poetic language works. Not so much the mythological structure or cultural memory, but seizing the moment sometimes in a surrealistic mode and giving a validity to man's personal experience. And through this limited experience and time frame, poetry expands into a universal mode of apprehending reality. In other words, instead of taking an archetype as a historical reality and anchoring thoughts into it, here the individual moment is experienced as an eternity. I believe with Rambau that poetry, like life, should either be intense or not at all. This is its relevance in our times. Today, the relevance of good poetry is how to keep the quality of human imagination alive because there are so many assaults on imagination.

SM: It must be gratifying for you to see that regional poetry has been given its due, thanks to the emphasis on ethnicity. Do you think that this is a changing fashion or something more enduring?

MA: No, I believe it is much more than a changing fashion. It seems to be the result of society's response to arts in general. A sort of return to roots. Alien modes may not be appropriate for apprehending your own reality. I am not saying that there is an Indian way of looking at literature or reality, but surely there is a qualitative difference in our approach, for instance, the way Gopinath Mohanty looks at love in the tribal context as distinguished from the portrayal of love in Henry Miller or D.H. Lawrence. Death, for instance, in the Western context is something unwelcome and to be kept away. But in a society where even a child is exposed to death, death does not happen as in a deodorised, isolated hospital room. There is something about time and the myriad symbolism that the common people use.

SM: You have at times been described, quite justifiably, as one of the foremost interpreters of India's tribal poetry. How did you get interested in the tribal culture in the first place?

MA: Well, it was many years ago when I was in the district of Sundergarh where the Rourkela Steel Plant is located. Many evenings, in the camp area, I would see that the tribals like the *Mundas* would return with songs on their lips, and these were mellifluous and very pleasing to hear. And when I made an attempt to understand, I thought they spoke to me as poetry that there was something very intimate, very personal and moving. Then I started collecting some of these poems. I've called them song poems because they are primarily meant to be sung, but they are also linked to ritual systems, sometimes to the naming of the birth of a child, a marriage, or a death. I learned the Santhali language during my days in Mayurbhanj.

SM: I understand that you did most of these translations under the Homi Bhaba Fellowship?

MA: In fact, I got time during that two-year Fellowship, from 1975-77. I've tried to collect those songs in order to systematise them. These songs are basically in two streams. One I call the life circle stream, beginning from the birth of a child to the funeral rites. The birth of the child is an occasion to invoke the blessings of the entire universe—the birds, beasts, flowers, and even the inanimate worlds. A

Santhali father looking for an alliance would describe his daughter as a flower in blossom, just as a Munda lover would describe his beloved as a Sal tree in blossom. Unlike us, there is an integrated vision among the tribals. No one knows about the first creator of these poems. Lines are always added and modified, but they remain part of one tradition.

SM: Given the threat of modernity, do you think that we are at the risk of idealising tribal life and culture?

MA: No, on the contrary, I'm deeply aware that it is easy to romanticise tribal life and culture because among the tribals also, there has been a lot of violence, there are occasional destruction of forests. But my attitude towards the tribals is not to treat them as another form of minorities. Perhaps there are certain universal characteristics in their psyche, their social life, which could be valuable to modern man. For instance, the whole tribal village looks upon itself as one unit at the time of a crisis, the entire village comes to one's rescue. So, it is a kind of community solidarity, where the individual is not like a speck of dust floating in the wind. That is one. And the other is an integrated vision that I've already spoken of. The ancestors are still relevant, the Gods are still relevant, other human beings are still relevant. And the third thing that we can learn from the tribals is that life is not just pleasure and pain, life is a journey. Of course, development is what the tribals certainly deserve, they must share in the national cake, they must not lead a life of deprivation, economic, educational, social. But we will be poorer by making the tribals a carbon copy of ourselves. You should look at the universalism in their culture for what is important for us.

SM: Today, in the overall scenario, when information technology and management seem to call the shots, what do you think is going to be the future of poetry?

MA: I know that this question is increasingly being asked, "What's going to be the fate of the written word in the age of cyber space and audio-visual media?" I believe that these new forms cannot supplant human dreams and imagination. They are not capable of creating alternative universes of imagination. I believe that the written word will survive. The structured world of the digital cyber space does not take into account human instincts and intentions.

SM: And finally, what would you say to the aspiring poet in India?

MA: Try to be yourself, try to be completely loyal to your own experience, try to hold on to your experience as much as you can to seek meaning from it. For a creative writer or artist, no meaning is ever given, it is always created!